Aby

Enjoy your Reading

WE

ARE

GODS

We are gods

Rev. Noel Maturlu
January 2009

We are gods

PREFACE

This book is a purely devotional and sincere expression of my personal understanding of the topic under discussion. It is not intended to be an academic script, which comprises different views on the topic. It is my desire that this book will help many to discover their true selves and enjoy their living here on planet earth.
-Noel Maturlu

We are gods

DEDICATION

To all gods - the children of the most high God

We are gods

THE GOLDEN ATTITUDE

Appreciate that you are a special creation; you are God's offspring. Know that God put His spirit in you the moment He created you. You already have the nature and character of God in you. And if you bear God's nature accept that you are indeed a god.

Be grateful that God created you because He desired you. He meticulously planned your living here on earth before you were born. Appreciate that you have been fashioned and sent in to this world for a special mission that involves improving life in a specific way. Upon completion of your mission on earth you will be recalled back home to your Heavenly Father.

Know that God's purpose for your life is revealed to you in a form of a burning desire. Because your desires are God's perfect will for you, believe that everything has been set to make them come true. Understand that you have everything you need to play your part in realizing your desires.

Remember that God want you to succeed because you are His project. Always trust His judgment and His good will as He channels His will through your desires. Be aware also that God reserves the right to execute his plans in your life without informing you in advance. But be assured that what ever circumstance He allows in your life is profitable to you and to others. Know that what ever you have been, what ever you are, and what ever you will be is in line with your Father's perfect plan.

Lastly, accept and appreciate that principally the above is also true for every other human being. So love, respect and serve all humanity with diligence for the glory of God our Father.

We are gods

TABLE OF CONTENTS

We are gods

INTRODUCTION

According to a recent report released by the World Institute for Development Economics Research at the UN University, 1% of the world adult population owned 40% of the world's wealth in 2000. Just think about this only 2% of adults owned more than 50% of the global wealth .The statistics revealed also that a mare 10% of grown men in the world owned a staggering 85% of the global wealth. That means a whooping 90% of us collectively owned a pitiful 15% of the world wealth. Perhaps even more depressingly it was revealed that 50% of the poorest adults collectively contributed barely 1% to the world wealth[1].

These figures unmask a sad reality that has been apparent throughout human history. In almost every society for many generations a small number of people happen to enjoy the life of prosperity. Very few people happen to enjoy their lives compared to the rest of the population put together. In the bible we are told that out of more than two million Israeli adults who left the Egyptian slavery only two of them (0.0001%) made it to the promised land of freedom and prosperity.

Of course I am not suggesting that material wealth by itself is a measure of prosperity. As you will learn throughout this book, to live a happy, fulfilled and prosperous life one need more than material wealth. But the truth remains that, irrespective of the fact that all of us (I mean all of us) having exactly equal opportunities, too few of us seem to live that deserving life. It seems too few people know the secret to prosperity.

I believe this is not supposed to be so. Every human being is the son of God by birth. And because of this the bible says every human being has a share of inheritance of our heavenly father's vast wealth. Allan Cohen the author of *Relax into Wealth* said

While some of us may complain about how little there is of this and that, the universe was created in absolute, utter, glorious, eternal,

---

[1] http://www.wider.unu.edu/events/past-events/2006-events/en_GB/05-12-2006/

non-stop, never-ending, over-the-top, knock-your-socks-off abundance. Not just enough more than enough. Extravagant, actually.

I find this to be very true. This is why I have dedicated my life to living this truth and helping those who are willing to do the same. I live to inspire people (including myself) to enjoy life of prosperity as our undisputable birthright. My desire is for whole of   humanity to realise true natural identity as masters of our destinies and indeed as co- creators of the world with our Father God. The purpose of this book is therefore to remind myself and my fellow human beings, regardless of our race or gender, that WE ARE GODS by nature.

OUR NATURE

I say you are gods and the children of the Highest God

God the Almighty

Understandably some of you consider the notion that we are gods unbelievable or crazy. Sadly this is because many of us have been made to believe that God the almighty is too holy, too powerful and too perfect to be likened to us mare mortal beings.

The truth is that God our Father is like us. He created us to be like Himself- equally creative and masters of our destinies in this world. All successful people accept this truth. And this is the one of the major reasons why they are successful in the first place. All high achievers- past and present have one thing in common- they accept the fact that prosperous living is both their birth right and their sole natural responsibility. They believe that God predestined them to live a prosperous life and that He has already deposited in them every resource they will ever need to achieve whatever they set their heart to do.

Successful people are just ordinary human beings born with imperfections. All of them faced equally difficult times at some point in their lives but still achieved extra ordinary results. These are the people we admire, respect and cherish the most- people in the names of Jesus Christ, King David, Solomon, Joseph, Abraham, Elijah, Paul the Apostle, Prophet Mohammed, Dalai Lama, Albert Eistein, Galileo Galilei, JF Kennedy, Martin Luther King Jr, Mahatma Ghandi, Mother Theresa, Nelson Mandela, TD Jakes, Joel Osteen, Bill Gates, Richard Branson, Oprah Winfrey, David Bekham, Benny Hinn, Barak Obama, Warren Buffet and many more.

Because there is a thin line between confidence and arrogance, in many occasions the confidence of these high achievers has been mistaken with arrogance or even with blasphemy. Tragically some risk their own lives by doing this.

Galileo Galilei is one example. He was tortured, imprisoned and excommunicated from the church community because he challenged a belief held by many at the time. Every body believed that the world was flat and that the sun was actually mobile- moving from the east to the west in a daily basis. But Galileo was convinced that the world was actually round. And contrary to a popular belief at the time (very popular in fact to the point that even biblical writers believed to be so)[1] Galilei found that the sun was indeed stationery and the world was mobile – orbiting around it. As a result of holding to his view Galileo's discovery finally changed not only his life for the better but also the life of all humanity.

Jesus Christ is another person whose faith in His own personality changed the cause of history. He was crucified because he – an ordinary human - called himself the child of God.

Many accepted Jesus as the genius, as the great teacher and as the man of peace. They loved him for his great humanitarian works. They applauded him for defending the weak and for his love for the poor. But they stumbled on his 'arrogance' and on his 'blasphemy' by claiming to be god.

But what Jesus believed was neither strange nor was it inflammatory. He reiterated what all sacred texts had since acknowledged. He did what every one of us is actually supposed to do- to publicly and confidently confesses that God the almighty is our Father. And that we are naturally gods.

In response to their claim, Jesus cited God the almighty's statement. In context God's key note speech to the leaders of their day said

"I say you are gods and the children of the Highest God. *I chose you to be leaders. I commissioned you to take charge of my people in my behalf .Your responsibility was to care for the weak and the destitute; defend the rights of the poor ; stand up for the powerless, and prosecute all those who exploit them...[2]*

Clearly in this text God Himself officially, publicly and proudly declared all human beings as His children and therefore gods. He delegated His authority to human beings to take care of all creation and each other.

In the book of Genesis God almighty is recorded saying that He created us to be like him- to bear his nature and character.[3]

Better Than Angels?

It is written

What are mere mortals (enosh), that you should think about them, human beings that you should care for them? Yet you made them only a little lower than God and crowned them with glory and honor. You gave them charge of everything you made, putting all things under their authority—the flocks and the herds and all the wild animals, the birds in the sky, the fish in the sea, and everything that swims the ocean currents[4].

To understand the weight of this text let us revisit the first sentence. Bible scholars tell us that this sentence as it appears in the original Hebrew text (Septuagint) should read as follows;

What is miserable fallen man (enosh), that you should still think about him? Who is the son of Adam that you still care for him?

According to Adam Clark Commentary, *Adam*, is the name given to man at his creation, and expresses his origin, and generic distinction from all other animals. *Enosh*, which signifies *sick, weak, or wretched*, was never given to him till after his fall. The *son of Adam* means here, any one or all of the fallen posterity of the first man.

To the psalmist it was stunning that human beings- even at their fallen, imperfect state- were still, by far, the most superior of all creations. This text confirms that God made us human beings just little lower than Himself -meaning only God our father is superior to us. No other creature is that close to God in superiority. That is why God gave us the authority to rule the world. He put the whole world under the control of human beings- not under the control of angels.

The word *angel* means *messenger,* or *servant.* I am not sure what type of creature angels are but what I know is that they are just spiritual servants of men. They are created (or sent) by God specifically to serve living human beings on earth. They are, by no means superior to us.

OUR CAPABILITIES

Knowing others is intelligence; knowing yourself is true wisdom.
Mastering others is strength, mastering yourself is true power

---

- Lao-Tzu

By harnessing our incredible creative ability human beings have achieved outstanding results. In the past few centuries though, human beings have made even astonishing scientific advancements. For example in his article *Future of science: 'We will have the power of the gods'* Roger Highfield quoting   Michio Kaku (the theoretical physicist Professor of the City College of New York) said;

"We human beings are entering an empowered new era. We have unravelled the molecule of life, DNA. And we have created a form of artificial intelligence, the computer. We are making the historic transition from the age of scientific discovery to the age of scientific mastery in which we will be able to manipulate and mould nature almost to our wishes."

Professor Kaku , believes that in the coming decades the following scientific advancements will reshape the way we live; cars that drive themselves, lab-grown human organs, 3D television, robots that can perform household tasks, eye glasses that double as home-entertainment centres, the exploitation of genes that alter human ageing and the possibility of invisibility and forms of teleportation.

Now why is it that we are seeing all these breath-taking scientific advancements now? Joel Garreau, author of Radical Evolution has given us a clue

"For the first time, our technologies are not so much aimed outward at modifying our environment in the fashion of agriculture or space travel; increasingly, technologies are aimed inward, at modifying our minds, our memories, our metabolisms, our personalities and our kids. And this is not in some distant, science-fiction future – this is now. What's shocking about this is that if you can do all that, you're

talking about humans becoming the first species to take control of their own evolution."

For a long time humans have been searching for answers from outside themselves. We have been conditioned to believe that the source of happiness, joy, fulfilment and prosperity is out there- from other people or material things. At last we have switched our attention toward the right direction- in our inside. And because of this we are now taping unto the unlimited potential within us.

According to Isaac Newton despite all these unprecedented scientific breakthroughs we have used just a minute fraction of our creative potential. Just before he died speaking of his amazing scientific discoveries Newton said

"I seem to have been only like a boy playing on the seashore and diverting myself in now and then finding a smoother pebble or prettier shell than ordinary, while the great ocean of truth lay all undiscovered before me."

It is believed that we have so far managed to utilise not more than 5% of our brain capacity. I believe as we learn more about ourselves and discover who we rally are, we will unearth our true massive untapped potential as gods. We will continue to uncover the ocean of truth and live the kind of life that those before us never even dreamt of.

Again, as Professor Kaku said *"We will have the power to animate the inanimate, the power to create life itself. We will have the power of gods. But will we also have the Wisdom of Solomon"*. Adding to this powerful statement I say that we already have -within us- the power of gods and the Wisdom of Solomon. What we need is to believe it, unearth it and tap unto it!

The case I am advocating is this: - we human beings -those still alive, those who ever lived, and those to be born- are gods. We have been endowed with natural divine creative ability to achieve what ever God puts in our hearts to achieve. We were created by God to bare His nature and share his character in order to fulfil his good will on earth.

Even in our imperfect state- whether we know it or not- we have full divine authority over all creation in this world! Beside God our Father no other creature in heaven above, on earth or in hell beneath can match our natural superiority!

If God Himself has never been ashamed to call us gods why should we? We are not ashamed to call snake's children what they are - snakes. No matter how small they might be. We proudly call chicken's children by the name that bares their true natural identity - chicken. Why should we -as children of God- be ashamed to call ourselves what we truly and naturally are- gods?

For those of us who are some how struggling in life we should take comfort from the achievement of others. If our fellow human beings have achieved that much we can also over come our own obstacles. If Bill Gates can accumulate more than $50bn surely we can, deservingly, earn enough money to sustain our families every month. If Jesus Christ walked on water we can walk on our fears and despair. If Joshua – a human being like me – through faith was able to stop the solar system for twenty four hours surely I also can stop the cycle of poverty in my own life. If Stephen Hawkins, a science genius can earn academic appraisals and make such incredible positive contribution to humanity despite his severe physical disability, every one can make a positive difference in our world.

If we can successfully send a man into space; if we can unravel the molecule of life and create artificial intelligence then we are undoubtedly capable of living in love, peace and harmony with each other!

THE GOLDEN BUDDHA

Recently I stumbled on an incredible story of a 900 year old golden Buddha located in one of the Buddhist temples in Thailand. It   is believed to be 10.5 foot tall   weighing over 2.5 tons of solid Gold and valued at nearly $196 million. But the golden Buddha's true value had never been so explicit through out.

When the Burmese were about to invade the city, the monks covered the Buddha with clay to keep their golden Buddha from being looted. The golden Buddha remained covered in clay for the next two centuries and was thought to be worth very little until 1957 when an amazing discovery was made by one of the monks.

On that eventful day a group of monks had to relocate 'clay' Buddha from their temple to a new location. During the journey the crane transporting the statue broke under the strain and crashed the clay Buddha to the ground. When one of the monks was examining the damage caused by the crash he noticed a light shining out from a crack in the clay.

Out of curiosity he started chipping away at the clay. After many hours of labour later, the monk discovered that the Buddha they believed to be made of clay was indeed made of precious solid gold.

We are made of pure spirit covered with biological clay- the body. Beneath these mortal bodies lies a pure God's nature – the spirit. Just like a hand gloves fits the shape and size of a hand, our bodies fit the size and shape of our souls.

But because our true valuable nature is hidden beneath the clay body many of us value ourselves much less than we actually are. But some of us, through the cracks caused by trials and tribulations of change in life have come to discover our true self worth.

We have read from the sacred text that God created the body of the first human being (Adam) from the earthly dust. But the body could not move, talk or reproduce because it was dead – it had no life (spirit) in it. It was until God pumped his spirit in the body that the first human became into being.[5]

That is to say we originate from eternity. We all entered the world through the body synthesized from the earthly biological clay. As we will see in the coming chapters our body sizes and shapes are designed specifically to enable us fulfil a specific purpose here on earth. When that mission is over we simply take off our biological body masks and return to where we came from –eternity. This process of taking off the biological jacket is what is popularly known as death. Death is not the end of life. Yes it is the end of human existence here on earth; but it is actually the beginning (or the continuation) of eternal life.

Many of us define ourselves and others on the basis of the distinctions of our biological bodies. We judge humanity by looking at outward physical attributes. We value one's personality by their skin colour, shape, size or gender. We calculate other peoples worth based on their behaviour, or by the content of their material possessions. All these do not reflect the true value of the real person inside each one of us.

To appreciate our true value we need to cut through these different types of earthly bodies. We must choose to ignore these temporal differences of ours and by using our spiritual forensic minds gaze hard enough through into the inner man. By doing so we will be able to see and appreciate the timeless truth that we are all the same- equally powerful, equally beautiful, equally valuable, equally lovely, equally peaceful and equally eternal spirits of God.

OUR PURPOSE

Heaven belongs to God our Father but He has given the earth to us to take full control of it

----

Psalms 115:16

God created us for a reason. Each and every human being is here for a specific timed mission. The duration and the quality of our living here on earth is directly proportional to the alignment to our life purpose. We will talk about individual life purpose   later, but let me stress that according to the sacred texts, God had a purpose for creating us humans.

God said let us make a human being- our child like us. Let us clothe him with an earthly body. So he can have complete authority and be responsible for the fish in the sea, the birds in the air, the cattle, and, yes, the Earth itself and every thing in and on it. So God created (male and female) human being according to His plan; resembling Himself, carrying His nature and ready to take charge of His business on earth. Then God affirmed them and said:"You now have full authority and responsibility over the earth and everything in it .So go ahead and be successful in every way, reproduce, fill the earth, take charge and be responsible for all other creatures on earth!"[6]

You see we have been created with the unimaginable incredible unlimited creative capabilities buried beneath our earthly vessels. Deep within ourselves lies pure and untapped potential to create and manage anything we can imagine or desire. This creative ability was invested in us for a reason – to enjoy our living here on earth as we take care of each other and the whole of creation.

The very reason we need a body is to enable us to live and carry out a specific mission for our Father here on earth; the mission that He himself- being a spirit - could not fulfil. Just like living in space requires special body jackets, a spirit needs physical body to operate in this world. In other words we are better suited to live and undertake certain tasks here on planet earth than God our father!

The sole purpose of creation is to relieve the creator from the duties that the creator either can't or don't want to do. Let me explain.

Cars were invented to help us human beings move from point A to point B faster than we could ourselves. I mean we needed to move faster, but because we couldn't we invented cars to do the job for us. Of course we are far more intelligent and superior than cars but we can not do what cars do. Like wise, God created the world and needed some one to manage it and in the process of doing that enjoy living in it.

Paul in the book of Galatians says we are all Children of God and heirs of His vast wealth. God not only expects, but enjoys seeing us living in freedom of abundance. This was His pleasurable and deliberate plan!

Prosperous creative ability is our birth right as children of God. We are not supposed to ask for it – it is already within us. He has already blessed us with all the resources we might ever need to meet his expectation. Our duty is to unearth and use these resources.

With this understanding I can boldly say that living in prosperity and enjoying our creative ability is supposed to be a normality not an exception! Good life littered with wellness, love, wealth, achievement and peace of mind was meant to come as standard not as extras. Every human being that embraces this truth inevitably lives a life of fulfilment.

OUR CHARACTER

Watch your thoughts; they become words. Watch your words; they become actions. Watch your actions; they become habits. Watch your habits; they become character. Watch your character; it becomes your destiny.

———————

Frank Outlaw

I know some of you are rightly asking yourself these questions; if indeed we are gods – created with all these creative powers for the purpose of managing the world why are we struggling in life? If we are truly children of a loving, wealthy generous God and heirs of His vast wealth here on earth then why there is much poverty in the world? If we truly possess the true nature of God- who is holy, righteous, peaceful and just why is it that the world is littered with unprecedented evils such as wars, inequality, sickness, terror and death?

To answer these legitimate questions we must first differentiate between the nature and the character (or behaviour) of God. Nature is who we are but character is how we are. Our lifestyle –how we live and relate to each other- is merely a display of character.

Nature   is an inborn or inherent quality. But behaviour is the manifestation of nature. Nature is like a seed and behaviour is like a harvest. In order for a seed to develop into a harvest it requires conducive resources and conditions .Just like it is possible to have a healthy seed and have poor harvest, it is possible to have perfect nature of God and have poor behaviour .

We get the nature of God from birth but we manifest His nature through wisdom. We do not need to make a conscious decision to receive the nature of God (to be born), but to manifest His nature (behave like God) we must make conscious deliberate decisions.

Who we really are in our inside is our natural self identity. But how we behave (or live) is our personality (or life style). Our identity is the product of nature but our personality is the product of nurture. Our true identity is an inherent (inborn) trait. I.e. we don't learn to become children of God we are born as such. Personality on the other hand is acquired. No one is born with a godly personality we- all must learn it.

For a deeper understanding let us examine the following text.

...if a father dies and leaves a wealthy inheritance for his young children, their wealth remains under trustees until they reach whatever age their father set. Even though they legally own all of their father's wealth those children are not much better off than slaves. This is because being immature they have to depend on the trustees for their freedom and provision until they grow up...[7]

Apostle Paul argues that although children of a wealthy father are naturally and legally wealthy, access to (manifestation of) their wealth is restricted until the children have reached a certain level of maturity. Children aren't allowed to enjoy their prosperity freedom until the time when they are capable of making conscious wise decisions by themselves. Although we are naturally children of God, we can not naturally manifest Godly behaviour unless we have come to a certain level of maturity.

Our Father expects us to develop wealth management capabilities before entrusting the wealth to us. In other words wealth is ready for us but we must be ready for the wealth. The amount of wealth we will be allowed to possess (manifest) at any one time will be proportional to our level of maturity.

To illustrate this point further let me give you two stories. One is that true recent story of a jungle girl and the other is that popular biblical story of a prodigal son.

The Jungle Girl

Ro Cham H'pnhieng, was eight years old when she disappeared in to the Cambodian jungle. On January 2007 -18 years after she disappeared Ro Cham then 27, was discovered after she was caught trying to steal food left under a tree.

When she was discovered Rocham was a half human half animal. She was naked and walking in a bending-forward position like a monkey. She was so skinny, shaking picking up grains of rice from the ground and could speak only three words - mother, father and stomachache.

Rocham found it difficult adjusting to life with humans. Her family's biggest fear was that she would escape back to the jungle because she was clearly baffled by her new surroundings. She hardly slept and mostly sat in a corner looking for means of escaping.

His father - a village policeman in Rattanakiri province, northern Cambodia, where the family live, said his daughter tried to escape several times but relatives had always been able to stop her. Finally, in October 2007 -ten weeks after being found- Rocham returned to the wilderness. It is believed that Ro ran away back to the jungle to find "her wild man" who was living with.

The Prodigal Son
As told by Jesus Christ[8]

There was once a wealthy man who had two sons. The younger said to his father, 'Father, I want my inheritance right now. So the father divided the property between them.

It wasn't long before the younger son packed his bags and left for a distant country. There, undisciplined and dissipated, he wasted everything he had. After he had gone through all his money, there was a bad famine all through that country and he began to hurt. He signed on with a citizen there who assigned him to his fields to slop the pigs. He was so hungry he would have eaten the corncobs in the pig slop, but no one would give him any.

That brought him to his senses. He said, 'All those farmhands working for my father sit down to three meals a day, and here I am starving to death. I'm going back to my father. I'll say to him, Father, I've sinned against God, I've sinned before you; I don't deserve to be called your son. Take me on as a hired hand.' He got right up and went home to his father.

When he was still a long way off, his father saw him. His heart pounding, he ran out, embraced him, and kissed him. The son started his speech: 'Father, I've sinned against God, I've sinned before you; I don't deserve to be called your son ever again.'

But the father wasn't listening. He was calling to the servants, 'Quick. Bring a clean set of clothes and dress him. Put the family ring on his finger and sandals on his feet. Then get a grain-fed heifer and roast it. We're going to feast! We're going to have a wonderful time! My son is here—given up for dead and now alive! Given up for lost and now found!' And they began to have a wonderful time.

All this time his older son was out in the field. When the day's work was done he came in. As he approached the house, he heard the music and dancing. Calling over one of the houseboys, he asked what was going on. He told him, 'Your brother came home. Your father has ordered a feast—barbecued beef!—because he has him home safe and sound.'

The older brother stalked off in an angry sulk and refused to join in. His father came out and tried to talk to him, but he wouldn't listen. The son said, 'Look how many years I've stayed here serving you, never giving you one moment of grief, but have you ever thrown a party for me and my friends? Then this son of yours who has thrown away your money on whores shows up and you go all out with a feast!'

His father said, 'Son, you don't understand. You're with me all the time, and everything that is mine is yours—but this is a wonderful time, and we had to celebrate. This brother of yours was dead, and he's alive! He was lost, and he's found!'"

These two stories highlight one important point. That it is possible to be naturally and legally blessed but live in poverty. They prove that it is possible to have the nature of righteousness but manifest an evil behaviour. Rocham was (and still is) a human being but she behaves like a monkey. The prodigal son was still the son of a wealthy person even when he was living as a pauper.

EVEN GODS MUST LEARN THROUGH MISTAKES

You cannot dream yourself into a character; you must hammer and forge yourself one.

James A. Froude

It has been proven that the fear of making mistakes is one of the major reasons people fail to achieve their much deserving success. This is because people literally hate making mistakes. In my view, the reasons why average people hate making mistakes is three fold.

Firstly many people link perfection to godliness and mistakes to Satanism. They believe that gods are always perfect. Secondly many believe that God's love is conditional. They think God loves (rewards) us only when we are perfect and hates (punishes) us when we show signs of imperfection.

The painful nature of mistakes is the third reason. All mistakes are by nature painful and costly. Because almost every one of us hates pain, we try to avoid mistakes when ever possible.

Making mistakes is part of a learning process. Oprah said;
Do the one thing you think you cannot do. Fail at it. Try again. Do better the second time. The only people who never tumble are those who never mount the high wire. This is your moment. Own it.

What average people don't understand is that godliness is the product of mistakes. They do not know that God ordained mistakes to be part of a learning process that installs godly character. We were born *to be* perfect. That means we were born imperfect. And as you probably know already perfection is the product of practise that involves making as many mistakes as necessary.

We all have to learn godly character. The bible says *though Jesus was the Son of God, yet he learned obedience by the things which he suffered*[9]. This proves that even Jesus was not born perfect. He had to learn through a painful process of trials and tribulations like all of us. He stayed in the womb for nine months like all of us; he was born, raised and behaved like any other kid. He was not born a genius - he was born with average intelligence but learnt to be what God intended him to be.

A one day old lion cub is naturally a lion. But it does not become a full grown lion from birth. It has to learn –through testing, trials and errors. God's children are no exception.

God's Love Is Unconditional

"...nothing can ever separate us from God's love. Neither death nor life, neither angels nor demons, nothing present, nor that is to come— not even the powers of hell can separate us from God's love. No power in the sky above or in the earth below—indeed, nothing in all creation will ever be able to separate us from the love of God that is revealed in Christ Jesus our Lord..) [10]

Although nature always determines our lifestyle our lifestyle does not always determine or nullify our true natural identity. By this I mean mistakes does not make one a son of a devil. Rocham as I write is behaving like a monkey but that does not qualify her for a monkey status; she is still a human being – a god. By sharing food and shelter with pigs the prodigal son did not turn into a pig. He was still a loved son of a wealthy father.

I have three lovely children. As a parent I expect children to fall down many times as they learn to walk and run. Falling does not diminish my love for the child. Instead it intensifies it to the point of encouraging and taking care of a fallen child.

Rocham's parents still love her as their daughter and still pray for her eventual safe return. The prodigal son still had a special place in his father even when he was living in deep poverty. That is why when he returned his father was so delighted to see him again.

God loves us unconditionally. He loves us with our mistakes. Our perverted behaviour does not make Him hate us because He knows that pervasiveness is a sign of immaturity. He does not condemn us because he knows all too well that making mistakes is the only way to maturity. He knows this because He as the creator of all things intended it to be that way!

In a nutshell mistakes have several advantages

Mistakes Are Destiny Indicators

Mistakes are indicators of our immaturity. If anything our mistakes show God our areas of weakness that still need fixing in order to make us become what He wanted us to be. Pain was meant by God to be a natural guide not as a tool for punishment. It is a beeper in our natural navigation system that tells us that we are heading towards the wrong direction. Once we are back on track the beeper stops.

Pain is a natural alarm that shows that something is wrong somewhere in our bodies that need fixing. Once that problem is fixed pain goes off. When you put your hand on a hot object you feel pain – meaning something is interfering with your normal functioning in your hand and therefore you should take your hand off. Once your hand is off pain subsides.

When ever there is smoke there must be fire. Whenever there is pain there must be a mistake. The feeling of pain in any area of our life – in a relationship , career, or in our finances - indicates that there is something in that area that needs fixing. Instead of complaining and being upset about it we must locate the fault and make the necessary amends.

Mistakes Are Blessings In Disguise

Every mistake is a blessing in disguise. I mean every mistake do come with an element of good and bad in one package. Successful people have a tendency of ignoring the bad element and focus on the good element of the mistake. The people who enjoy life to the full know that God's best gifts come wrapped up in ugly boxes called mistakes. When they discover a mistake they know that inside it there is a precious gift from God. So instead of feeling guilty and worried they take time to unwrap it and enjoy the gift.

The amazing discovery of a true value of a golden Buddha in a story I shared with you earlier was a result of someone's mistake. The crane driver crashed the 'clay' Buddha to the ground and caused huge cracks that exposed its golden nature. We were born valuable individuals loaded with valuable talents buried beneath us. But we need some situations – sometimes very unprecedented painful situations - to cause huge cracks in our personalities in order to reveal our true self.

God do conceal our precious destinies inside disabilities and other seemingly unfortunate life scenarios to hide it away from our enemies. He does so to fool the potential looters of our dreams until the appointed time and place. A perfect example is that of Joseph[11].

Joseph had a dream of becoming a star. Having learnt of his dream his brothers sold Joseph to slave traders who eventually sold him to an Egyptian army official named Potipher. Joseph was later jailed after he was falsely accused of an attempted sexual assault on Potipher's wife.

All these unfortunate situations revealed extraordinary leadership skills Joseph possessed. It was in jail that his talent was discovered. From jail Joseph- an inmate slave serving term for 'sex offences'- was appointed to be an Egyptian Prime Minister.

God disguised his destiny in a nasty identity of a *slave* and *convicted sex offender*. He allowed a catalogue of mistakes made by his brothers and by the Potiphers to hide his true identity as the future Egyptian Prime Minister. I am very convinced that if God had not done this, Joseph's political enemies would have had him deported or assassinated.

Let me give you one more biblical example.

King David committed one of the most terrible mistakes any human being can possibly make. He had an affair with one of his soldier's wife- Bathsheba. Because he wanted to marry her David killed Uriah her husband by deliberately sending him to a dangerous battle front. Although he succeeded in marrying Bathsheba David's integrity as a leader was terminally diminished and eventually lost his position. To make the situation even worse David's first born with his new wife died shortly after birth. But out of this terrible mess something wonderful happened.

David had a life long desire to build a wonderful temple for his God. Because his hands were too bloody, God promised David to raise him a son that will carry out his ambitious project. Surprise, surprise, that child turned out to be Solomon – arguably the most handsome, the wisest, the wealthiest and the most successful human being ever lived. Although King David had more than one wife God chose Bathsheba to mother Solomon!

No one loves making mistakes deliberately. This is because no human being in his/her rational mind loves inflicting self pain deliberately. People make mistakes either unknowingly or as a desperate attempt to ease pain.

Choice is a preferred option that is expected to give the desired result. Sometimes people make wrong choices because they had limited options and time available at the time of decision making. But all people in their right mind make choices after they have been convinced that the choice they are making is the right choice in their judgement. Meaning the choice they are making will hopefully give them what they want. And always what people really want is to ease pain or improve a life of their own or some body else's.

So regardless of the results of our choices our intentions behind those choices is always good- to make the situation better.

The point I am making is this regardless of our failures –as a human race and as individuals -we are still gods. God's perfect plan for our destiny took our failures into account. I am confident that He, fuelled with unfailing love, is working in us to perfect us.

All successful people know that failure is part of success. All of them without exception believe that no one can succeed without failing. That is why they are neither terrified nor discouraged by mistakes. One of these people who know this secret of success is Alfred Adler who said the following;

What do you first do when you learn to swim? You make mistakes, do you not? And what happens? You make other mistakes, and when you have made all the mistakes you possibly can without drowning - and some of them many times over - what do you find? That you can swim? Well - life is just the same as learning to swim! Do not be afraid of making mistakes, for there is no other way of learning how to live!

LEARNING HOW TO LIVE

One day a man was walking through the shopping centre with his son. As they were passing outside the bike store they saw a nice bike on display. His son had desired this kind of bike for along time so they were delighted to have finally found it and were ready to buy and peddle it home.

They had expected to be given the bike in a complete drive away state- like the one that was on display. After making payment they were disappointed to be handed one big sealed box instead. They learnt then that they wouldn't be able to cycle their new bike straight away because it had to be assembled first. A replica bike they saw was for display only. As they later discovered each new bike came in a box and buyers were responsible for putting it together.

Although the man was pretty good in cycling and had a general knowledge of bikes he had never tried to assemble a new bike from scratch by himself. But since he was a Do-It-Yourself fanatic he resolved to take the challenge. He also invited his son to join him.

Inside the box they found three important things; parts, tools and the manual.

The manual had the instructions on how to assemble, how to use and how to maintain the bike. It also had important customer service contacts in case they needed any help. More importantly the manual had a nice picture of the bike- exactly the way it should look like after it has been successfully assembled. This same picture was also displayed outside the carrier box. After many trials and errors together with a help from customer service personnel, they were able to assemble the bike successfully.

Our life is like a new bike. We do not come as complete or perfect individuals. We come in a box in a form of an embryo. Before we can be fully functional and enjoy our destined life we must be assembled- we must be put together.

God starts to assemble us in the womb from the point of conception. He putts us together by using our destiny as a guide. Our destiny is a picture of ourselves in a perfect form. It is that picture of our selves exactly the way he wants us to look like and live like when we are fully matured.

After birth God continues to unpack and assemble us with a help of our parents or guardians. As children we depend heavily on parents and guardians to assemble us. But as we grow up the responsibility gradually shifts from the parents and guardians to ourselves.

As adults we become fully responsible for our own lives. To live a fulfilled life we are supposed, with a divine help, to put ourselves together according to our destiny vision.

Destiny Vision is the realisation of own destiny. It is having a clear vision of who were you meant to be; it is to understand and accept your life purpose; it is the discovery of your true self.

When you were conceived God put a copy of your destiny in you. But as a child you were unable to understand it without help. It is difficult to discover your destiny because, unlike the bike box, your destiny is not printed on your body- it is printed in your heart. You need to learn how to search and listen to your heart to understand it.

God has his customer service centres close to us all the time in a form of mentors, teachers, authors and psychologists to mention but a few. We all need this help. This is why you have this book in your hands now- to learn how to discover your true self.

DEVELOPING YOUR SELF IMAGE

Who Do We Think We Are Determines Our Behaviour

Self image (or self awareness) is our perception of our own self identity. It is our awareness of who do we think (or believe) we are. While personality is not always the reflection of our true identity, it is always the reflection of our self image. By this I mean our lifestyle is always consistent with who do we think we truly are. If we think we are monkeys we will behave like monkeys. If we think we are meant to be poor we will expect no more than poverty and therefore live in lack.

Rocham believes she is a monkey that is why she is behaving like a monkey. She feels comfortable to be among the monkeys in the jungle. She enjoys a monkey life style even if she is truly human.

The value we put on ourselves determine how others will treat us. In other words how others treat us gives us a clue on how we treat ourselves. The prodigal son put his value below the value of a pig no wonder every one treated him as such. He also saw himself as a sinner servant who does not deserve to be called the son of a wealthy man. No wonder he lived in poverty until he changed his self image. His lifestyle changed as soon as he came back to his senses and realised who he truly was.

Few years ago I heard a voice deep into my heart saying "in the next few days you will have some money. Buy yourself a Mercedes Benz". We had just moved to England from Africa. My wife and I were both jobless and drowning in the pool of debts. So driving a Mercedes Benz in England was unthinkable. That is why even after actually getting enough money to buy one I settled for a used Renault and sent the rest of the money to an orphanage in Africa.

But I felt really bad on my inside. I was not happy with letting myself down. For many months I felt guilty for settling for less than I truly deserved. After months of conviction I was convinced that as the child of God I deserved the best. I vowed to make amends and follow my heart.

It had been my life long desire to drive a Mercedes and own a house in England. But the desire had since died. Suddenly my passion came alive and I was ready to hope again. Within few months all my desires were fulfilled. I bought my Mercedes and owned my first house.

The world around us is a mirror that reflects our self image. Our world is not to anyone's fault but ours. It is the way it is because it has adjusted itself to fit our self image. If we want it to change all we need to do is to change the way we see and value ourselves.

FEELING GOOD ABOUT YOURSELF

You cannot be lonely if you like the person you're alone with

---

Dr. Wayne W. Dyer

Self feeling (or self esteem) is how we feel about ourselves in response to our self image. Self feeling is how much we like ourselves after seeing ourselves in our own minds.

Basically there are two types of self feeling- positive (good) self feeling and negative (bad) self feeling. We either feel good about our selves or we feel bad. We either love who we think we are or we hate.

Generally speaking self feeling is the reflection of the gap between who do we think we are (self image) and who we want to be (ideal self). If your self image is less than your ideal self you feel bad about your self. But if your self image matches your ideal self you feel good about your self.

I said earlier that our behaviour is a direct reflection of our self image. This is because our self image determines how we feel about our selves. And how we feel about our selves determines how we behave. In other words if we feel bad about ourselves we will behave badly. If we feel good about ourselves we will behave in a positive way. It is impossible to feel good about yourself and hate anyone at the same time. Hate and love can not occupy our heart at the same time.

Francois De La Rochefoucauld said it best; *The confidence which we have in ourselves gives birth to much of that which we have in others.*

YOUR SELF IDEAL

Let every man be respected as an individual and no man idolized

_____

Albert Einstein

Self ideal is the way we would like to be. We all have our own self ideals. We all have our own preferred personality. Some would like to be doctors; some would like to be air hostesses, soldiers, politicians, preachers, business men and so forth. The difference between self image and self ideal determines our self esteem. I mean the kind and intensity of our self esteem is proportional to the difference between our self image and our self ideal.

In reality our self ideal (what we want to be) is not always what we ought to be. Some times (or many times I should say) our ideal self is just a copy of some one's personality. For example one loves to be an actor but actually was meant to be a lawyer. That is why most of us still feel uncomfortable with ourselves (or achieve temporal satisfaction) even after we have matched our ideal self.

A negative self feeling could be due to a wrong self image, wrong ideal self or both. But which ever the case self feeling is always real. Whether it is true or false self image always generate a real self feeling that eventually determines our behaviour! It is like watching a movie.

Say for example you are watching a scary movie; the scary feeling that is being generated in your mind by the movie is real regardless of the fact that the movie is based on a real story or fiction. Likewise the picture of whom you think you are whether it reflects your true self or not will provoke a real feeling in your mind.

Who other people think we are is mainly the extension of our self image. We have a tendency to believe that because we think we are ugly then every one thinks we are ugly. Because of this we behave ugly. And because we act ugly, lo and behold, the world knows we are ugly and respond to us accordingly.

Ten out of twelve Israeli spies who went to scout the Promised Land were terrified by the giants they saw there. Because they saw themselves as inferior as grasshoppers they believed the giants also saw them as such. In reality they had no way to prove their argument. What they did was placing their own self image in the minds of the giants. In truth they were terrified by their own inferior image[12].

In summary the reason why there are much evil and lack in the world is that the world is full of immature baby gods. The world, sadly, is littered with people with negative self image and terrible low self esteem. As baby gods rise into maturity we will see the level of evils drop and the level of prosperity rise accordingly. What is required is to learn how to grow unto maturity. And that is what the following topic is all about- to help people raise their self esteem and be ready to behave like mature gods.

HOW SELF IMAGE IS DEVELOPED

When the character of a man is not clear to you, look at his friends

---

Japanese Proverb

We all come to this world without the knowledge of who we really are. We form (or acquire) our self image from the sources outside ourselves. It is like looking at the mirror. Since we can not see our own faces it is impossible to know how our faces look like except by either people's descriptions of us or by looking ourselves on the mirror.

Ordinary people pick their self image from nurture. By nurture I mean the combination of our upbringing and the associations we continue to form as we live. The way we are brought up – the words we hear about us, the treatment we receive, and the observations we make as kids all play a major part in the formation of our self image.

As children we tend to believe everything that we hear. So if we grew up hearing somebody telling us that we are stupid we are likely to believe that we are actually stupid. If we grew up in a poverty stricken environment we are likely to believe that we were created to be poor. Like wise if some one who meant so much to us told us when we were kids that we are ugly (or treated us as such) we are likely to develop an ugly self image. No wonder statistics show that our upbringing is to blame for most of evil behaviour in our society today.

Even at adult age what we continuously learn from close family members, teachers, religious leaders, celebrities, politicians, and from the media contribute enormously in the formation of both our self image and our self ideal.

Unfortunately the self image we generate from nurture (I call it nurtural self image) is always imperfect for one particular reason. It is formed from distorted or limited information about our true self. This is because nurtural agencies have no access to our true inner self.

At best, nurtural sources can only 'see' our visible qualities. So their description of us is normally based on the general information gathered from their observation of our visible physical qualities, from our behaviour and/or from (mostly outdated) historical data. The world has no way of determining our self worth other than by what they know about us. What they know about us is mainly as a result of what we choose to display to the world through our behaviour- how we talk, walk, dress, eat, and so forth.

At worst nurtural self image is based on distorted or opinionated information that aim at deliberately controlling human behaviour by installing a negative self image. One example of this is a traumatic negative image that was installed in the minds of black people by slave masters.

During the dark ages of slavery Christian slave owners used distorted facts from the bible to make black people believe that they are beasts and therefore inferior to white people. This lethal mental venom - preached publicly and enthusiastically from the church pulpits and from all social and political platforms- aimed at enslaving black people for generations. This inferior self image that has been successfully passed on from generation to generation is largely responsible for much social deprivation among black people wherever they can be found around the globe to date!

It is always easier to free people from slavery than to free slavery from people. Although it has been more than two hundred years since the abolition of physical slavery black people still suffer from mental slavery. We still lack self confidence at the face of the world because we see and believe that we are not as good as people of other races. Our desire for excellence and elegance is comparatively blunt because we still believe we are deservingly less worthy.

The point I am trying to make here is that no one in this world has the ability to know the true self of others except God the creator. From the point of conception our father places the true copy of the image of each person's true destiny in the spirit. But the destiny is never clear to the individual until he/she is mature enough to be able to study and understand it.

Let me be absolutely clear on this; if you do not know your true self no body else does! So trying to pass on the impossible task of describing your true self image to others is wastage of your valuable time. Remember we were given time to only do what is important to us. Trying to discover and tell other people's destinies is definitely not one of those important things!

YOUR TRUE SELF

Today you are You, that is truer than true. There is no one alive who is Youer than You

_____

Dr. Seuss

No one has ever been, is or will ever be like YOU. In his best selling book, *The Purpose Driven Life,* Rick Warren says *"DNA molecules can unite in an infinite number of ways. The number is 10 to the 2,400,000,000^{th} power. That number is the likelihood that you'd ever find somebody just like you. If you were to write out that number with each zero being one inch wide you'd need a strip of paper 37,000 miles long. To put this in to perspective, some scientists have guessed that all the particles in the universe are probably less than 10 with 76 zeroes behind it, far less than the possibilities of your DNA. Your uniqueness is a scientific fact of life."*

In reality true self image is a compound of nature and nurture.

By nature I mean a spiritual material we gathered from our spiritual heavenly parent (God). The spirit contains the breath of God (or life itself), the blue print of destiny and the ability to communicate with God our father. As said a foretime, no one have access to the spirit except the bearer (the soul).

Nurture (or physical body) entails genetic material we gathered from our biological parents together with culture, beliefs, norms and attitudes we glean from our environment. This includes things like body size, shape, tastes, gender, race, talents, and intelligence.

The body, unlike the spirit is physical and temporal. It is designed to carry out the soul's divine destiny. In other words the body is an instrument of destiny- it is a destiny tool box.

It is true that we are all the same, but it is also true that we are different and distinct. I mean we all have our similarities and our differences. For example we all have a spirit and a body. Our spirits came from our Father. Our bodies were made by God from the same clay material. Therefore we basically have same needs; we all need wellness, love, wealth, achievement and peace of mind.

But we are also different in identity and purpose. We are all unique in our genetic wiring. Each of us has a distinctive DNA – a biological material that is responsible for our unique shape, size and tastes.

Although we all need (to receive and give) love we differ in what we are willing to receive love from or give love to. Even if we all need food we differ in the kind and amount of food we prefer.

YOUR UNIQUE LIFE PURPOSE

God has given each of us our 'marching orders'. Our purpose here on Earth is to find those orders and carry them out. Those orders acknowledge our special gifts

---

Soren Kierkegaard

God created each human being for a unique purpose. We are here on earth for a specific task meant to be accomplished at a certain time period and place. Our nurture is a tool that shapes us for our life purpose. Put it differently, the very reason why we differ in shapes, sizes and tastes is because we have different destinies. Our genetic and cultural qualities are designed distinctively to suit God's unique purpose for our lives.

Our true self image is the totality of our identity and destiny. You are unique in every sense- unique in identity, character and purpose. So the idea of trying to be like every body else is not going to work. You were born a unique person so live your unique life by fulfilling your unique purpose.

I say every body is unique in every way. The idea that every body must live in a certain way is not practical. Every body was born unique and every body will surely die as unique. So let us allow each individual to enjoy their unique lives and fulfil their destinies.

Of course this does not mean we should live our own unique lives in the expense of others. The freedom to live our unique lives demands respect of others. By respect I mean exercising our rights of living our unique life without preventing others from exercising their rights to do the same.

When we live a life that is consistent with our true self we will feel happy, secure and prosperous. Acting others personality drains our joy and energy. Linda Berens said *"In our understandings and research about personality, we have come to recognize that to behave in ways not consistent with one's inborn pattern takes a tremendous amount of energy. In fact, it is highly related to stress.*

Temperament and type dynamics theory states we have favourite abilities that help us meet our psychological needs. These are specific to each temperament. When we get to use these "intelligences," we not only tend to excel, we also feel good about ourselves and are energized".

The awareness of true self image (or the discovery of self) is what I call wisdom. Others call maturity or new birth. In the next chapter we will start to learn how to discover our true self; how to become wise; how to mature; we will learn how to be born again!

UNDERSTANDING YOUR TRUE SELF

There are two great days in a person's life -- the day we are born and the day we discover why

_____

William Barclay

The greatest discovery is the discovery of self. Jesus questioned the wisdom of discovering the world and lose the sense of who you are in the process. But we have seen this happening time and again. As I mentioned in earlier chapters humans have managed to travel trillions of miles in to the space for exploration missions but have failed to discover their true self. Truly, as G.K. Chesterton said, *the self is more distant than any star.*

The source of wisdom is curious exploration. To discover ourselves we must seriously explore ourselves. "You have", said Alan Alda , "to leave the city of your comfort and go into the wilderness of your intuition. What you'll discover will be wonderful. What you'll discover is yourself". In other words you must loose yourself to find yourself.

Remember I said no one knows your true self except God your Father. So the discovery of self is impossible without His help. To get His help we must learn how to talk to Him. We must learn how to use what I call Spiritual Navigation System that He installed in us.

SPIRITUAL NAVIGATION SYSTEM

The intellect has little to do on the road to discovery. There comes a leap in consciousness, call it intuition or what you will, and the solution comes to you and you don't know how or why

---

Albert Einstein

As the name suggests, Spiritual Navigation System is a spiritual mechanism that helps us communicate with our heavenly Father. It is also known as the Spirit of God or Holy Spirit. Others call it instinct, intuition, hunch, inspiration or simply heart.

Basically the Spiritual Navigation System (SNS) is like a receiver that receives (picks) spiritual signals from the heavenly satellite and translates those signals into pictures and words that can be understood by our minds. The Holy Spirit is able to do this because he is present both in heaven – at the source of all intelligence and here on earth in every living heart[13].

During the old bible days God the Father gave some people a special privilege to communicate with Him and be able read other people's destinies. These people- popularly known as mediums, prophets, or priests- were given special training on how to use the Spiritual Navigation System.

In those days people had no other choice but to travel to specific places where prophets and priests could be consulted. If you lived in those days and had no access to one of these holy people (unless, of course, you were one of them) you had no access to the information regarding your destiny.

The disciples of Jesus achieved extraordinary results in their lives because they received a special, full, premium package of grace at the day popularly known as Pentecost[14]. The very reason Jesus Christ ordered this premium package of grace for his protégés is because he wanted them to perpetuate the special work he started during his three and a half years of mission here on earth. But not every one needs this special premium package of wisdom to be able to live a fulfilled life. This is because not every one is destined for this special, premium mission.

All of us are entitled to a simple, basic standard gracious exposure to the SNS. The system of just a chosen few to have basic wisdom was not meant to last for ever. God through Joel, one of those prophets, said

"The time is coming when I will put my spirit in to the heart of every living human being, and every one- yes every one – will be able to communicate directly with me, dream their dreams, prophesy about their own destinies and see visions for their future"[15]

The arrival of Jesus Christ opened the door for a new era of divine communication (also called New Testament). Gods plan for this new era is to gradually phase out the importance of prophets and priests. He wants every human being to be able to communicate with him directly – any time, anywhere. He intends to inscribe His principles, laws and instructions directly into the hearts of men.[16]

Talking to a Samaritan lady , Jesus announced the arrival of the time when prophets , priests or temple (church) visit was no longer necessary as a means of divine communication (also known as worship)[2] . Jesus said because God is spirit He was interested in seeing each and every one of His children talk to Him through their spirits in order to get true and authentic information from Him.[17]

---

[2] *This does not mean that God no longer uses prophets to communicate His message to the people. I believe God still uses prophets to communicate His message that is aimed at a group of people collectively. As for the individualised, personal specific messages God is interested in talking to individuals directly. God may use a third party to confirm the news delivered by the Holy Spirit rather than breaking the news. Also this does not mean that places of worship are now utterly useless. I believe the position of places of worship is vital in two ways. Firstly I believe places of worship like all prophets have the responsibility to teach and encourage people how to use the SNS by themselves. And Secondly I believe places of worship should be centres for care of the needy in the community.*

The day Jesus died the partition that separated the holy of holies – a place in the only Jerusalem temple exclusive to the high priest - gave way. This was an explicit symbol that a new era of communication with God our Father had truly begun.

Apostle Paul in the epistle to Titus also reiterated that the grace- the spirit of God that is able to teach all men   how to enjoy living in this present world - has now been made available to every living soul.[18] Meaning every one of us now has access to divine information. You do not need to be a special person or join a certain religion to be able to tap unto this extraordinary intelligence.

Every human has the SNS installed within. But special knowledge is required to enable one to use it and benefit from its valuable services. The ability to know how to understand and use the SNS is enables to tap into the divine intelligence. As Oprah Winfrey said *the ability to follow your instincts takes you to the source of true wisdom.*

The SNS enables us not only to understand our true self but also helps us fulfil our life purpose. So the level of success by large extent depends on our exposure to the SNS. This explains why other individuals achieve extraordinary results and others don't.

DESIRE: THE LANGUAGE OF GODS

Follow your instincts. That's where true wisdom manifests itself.

Oprah Winfrey

Paul[19] says God directs both our will and our actions in order to fulfil His pleasurable purpose in this world. God through Jeremiah said *"my best desire for man kind is to give each and every human being the desires of their heart[20]*. King David also said that God gives us the desires of our heart[21].

What these statements mean in truth is that God not just fulfils our desires but He actually causes us to desire. Every thing any human being will ever need at any time has been made available in the infinite store house. But no one receives anything from the infinite store hose unless one desires it. So God chooses what to give us by simply causing us to desire it - by sending the loving, pleasurable signal to our hearts through the SNS.

So desire is the proof that what we desire is the will of God for our life. Simply put you will know whether what you desire is the will of God for your life or not by how you feel about it.

THE DYNAMICS OF DESIRE

Desire is an exciting feeling generated by a dominant exciting thought.

Desire is an earnest longing. It is that persistent, stubborn craving for something not under our possession. Desire is that thing you choose to commit your full self to get it. It is what Sheila Graham calls *'...an exuberance that erupts through the skin and joins the energy that created the world.'*

Desire is our **EMPIRE** – an acronym for Exciting Mental Picture of Imminent Reality. A desire is that thing we do not have physically but it has occupied our minds in such a way that it keeps on manifesting itself in our actions. It is falling in love with an imminent future.

God is made of good and love. I mean good and love is God's DNA. So every thing that comes from Him must be good and lovely. If you find anything good, exciting and long lasting, James the brother of Jesus Christ says, it must have dropped from God your Father[22].

Because God is the spirit (he can not be seen by human eye) no human being has ever seen Him. We can not communicate with God by using physical means like words (spoken or written) or gestures. The only way to communicate with Him is by using spiritual language -through thoughts and feelings.

Thoughts are mental pictures of realities that exist in the intangible (spiritual) world. Every thing we can think of- though unseen by naked eyes- actually exists. So thinking is seeing things in the spiritual realm; it is surfing the Spiritual Website - literally.

A feeling is a response to thoughts. It is our reaction to what we are seeing in the spirit realm. Just like an exciting movie generates an excitement equivalent to watching a real live event, thoughts generate feelings exactly the same way as seeing or experiencing things (that we are thinking about) in a physical reality. This is because our minds can not differentiate between a thought and physical reality.

Love is a feeling generated by a lovely thought. Desire is an exciting feeling generated by a dominant exciting thought.

Experts tell us that we think in pictures. I believe God speaks in mental pictures too. His presence in this world can only be felt and expressed in our hearts through love – thinking of lovely things. Therefore the presence of love in our hearts is an absolute proof that God lives in our hearts.

Our desire is an indication that what we desire is our imminent perfect gift from God. For this reason nothing from heaven or earth can stop us from attaining and retaining what we love

In the natural world we have five senses; sense of sight, touch, smell, hearing and sense of taste. Emotion is a spiritual sense. Others call it emotional intelligence. By studying our feelings we can tell in general terms the nature of circumstances coming our way and how soon.

The nature of the feeling indicates that what triggers the feeling is coming. The intensity of the feeling indicates how soon that which triggers a feeling is likely to occur. The stronger the feeling the sooner it will happen.

As said above desire is an absolute proof that the thing you desire is coming your way. A desire for a Mercedes Benz for example is an absolute proof that it is on its way. It is a confirmation that a Mercedes has left the spirit world and it will arrive soon. Like wise fear is an absolute proof that what you fear is on its way.

Sometimes it is difficult to trace what triggers the feeling but you can always tell something good or bad is coming by how you feel. A bad feeling tells you something bad is coming and vice versa.

YOUR STRONGEST DESIRE IS YOUR TRUE SELF

If you love it you own it

In the same way you can discover your true self by observing your strong dominant feelings. You can know your true values by identifying your dominant feelings that drives your core life. Your true destiny must provoke love in your fibre. When ever you think about your life purpose or dream career it must exited you. This is because every thing that is given by God must be desirable. This includes your destiny.

The very reason why you must feel good about your destiny is because it must be in harmony with your true self. It is like wearing a pair of shoes that fits your size. A relationship or career that causes you constant pain indicates that it was not meant for you. It is like wearing a pair of shoes that does not match your size.

If I have to tell you the secret to creative success it will be this one- desire! We always get what we desire. Every one who have ever succeeded (and I mean every one who has ever achieved success deliberately) desired to succeed. All geniuses, all great business men and women, all great athletes, all great leaders' thinkers and all great humanitarians loved what they achieved. Most of them discovered their passion very early in their lives and dedicated all their lives in doing just that.

If you love it you own it. Allan Cohen put it better by saying

> *"You own what you own not by money, paper or force, but by your love for it and your connection to it. If something is deeply imbedded in your soul, it belongs to you. It comes to you and adheres to you by your appreciation and right use of it.*
>
> *While it appears that external rules govern who owns what, the prevailing law is the Right of Consciousness. If you are trying to attract a job, living situation, or life partner, your thoughts and feelings must be a march to it. You must love*

it, know you deserve it, and hold a vision for healthy, joyful use of it. Then and only then will it come to you, and without struggle or strain. You don't have to fight for it; you just have to be one with it.

If you are joined with something you truly deserve by your mental, emotional, and spiritual alignment with it, it is yours by universal law and no one can interfere... Justice is always being accomplished by the power of intention. Found yourself in universal principle, and everything you want and deserve will come to you and stay with you by the virtue of love". [23]

Steve Jobs the Apple Computers co-founder and CEO summed up even better this way

"You've got to find what you love, and that is as true for work as it is for your lovers. Your work is going to fill a large part of your life, and the only way to be truly satisfied is to do what you believe is great work, and the only way to do great work is to love what you do. If you haven't found it yet, keep looking, and don't settle. As with all matters of the heart, you'll know when you find it, and like any great relationship it just gets better and better as the years roll on. So keep looking. Don't settle."

DO WHAT YOU LOVE TO SERVE OTHERS

The meaning of life is to give life meaning

Ken Hudgins

Writing to his students Apostle Paul said

> *Now I commend you to our marvellous God and to his teaching that can make you into what he wants you to be and give you everything you could possibly need. As you so well know, I've never fancied anyone's wealth or fashion for free. I have worked hard for all my needs and for the needs of my family and staff. In everything I've done, I have demonstrated to you how necessary it is to work for the purpose of serving people - not for the purpose of exploiting them. Please always remember the words of our Lord Jesus: 'It is more rewarding to serve than to be served'.*[24]

Serving is solving a problem in exchange of a reward. Simply put, sound living is a reward for service. We were created to serve one another. Each one of us was created for a purpose of improving life in a particular way. The quality of one's life is in proportion to the quantity and quality of one's service.

The secret to wealth is to serve the people that can pay you well and to pay the people that serve you well. But the secret to a happy life is to serve the people that can not pay you.

Oprah Winfrey is one of the people I greatly admire. She is the richest black person alive. She is also the richest self made billionaire woman in America. The reason I have mentioned her is not only because she is rich but because of how she became rich. Oprah is extremely wealthy because she believes in serving people. Her life philosophy goes like this

The key to realizing a dream is to focus not on success but significance.. I've come to believe that each of us has a personal

calling that's as unique as a fingerprint… and that the best way to succeed is to discover what you love and then find a way to offer it to others in the form of service, working hard, and also allowing the energy of the universe to lead you.

If you want to enjoy sound living ask your self these questions

1. What is my best natural abilility?
2. What do the trusted people think is my best natural ability?
3. What career would I like to follow if I was guaranteed to have every thing I will ever need?
4. How can I serve as many people as possible by following the career I would like to follow if I was guaranteed to have every thing I will ever need?
5. What problem concerns me the most in this world especially in my vicinity?
6. Using all my best available means how can I be part of the solution for the above problem?
7. If I was sure that I have only one year to live what would I do to make lasting improvement in the lives of others in this world.

The answer for these questions is your life purpose. By fulfilling it you are guaranteed every thing you will ever need and many times more here on earth and in the world to come!

THE CREATIVE POWER OF GODS

Whatever the mind can conceive and believe, the mind can achieve

---

Napoleon Hill

To create is to translate own thought or imagination into a tangible reality

The bible tells us that God created the world by saying. For example we read; *And God said, Let there be light: and there was light*[25]. According to Strong's Dictionary the Hebrew word *ama* that has been translated as *say* in the text also means to *think, determine, desire, demand* or *command*.

We can therefore paraphrase the text this way; *"And God desired light; and there was light".*

John the beloved disciple of Jesus says

In the beginning was the Word, and the Word was with God, and the Word was God. He was with God in the beginning. Through him all things were made; without him nothing was made that has been made. In him was life, and that life was the light of men ...He was in the world, and though the world was made through him, the world did not recognize him...The Word became flesh and made his dwelling among us.[26]

Again according to Strong's Dictionary the Greek word *logos* translated as *Word* in the above text also means *the inward intention underlying the speech act, motive, thought,* or *desire*. If we substitute the word *Word* for *desire* the above scripture can also be paraphrased as follows;

In the beginning God had a desire. The desire had God's creative power in it. Every thing was created through and by God's desire. This very desire of God became a human being in the form of Jesus Christ and lived among men. Although he was the source of life, many did not appreciate Jesus as such because his divine nature was concealed in his flesh and he lived like any other human being ...

All these words have one thing in principle -*thought* or *imagination*. That is to say God created the world by the power of imagination. When God wanted anything He first thought about it. He then kept that thought in the mind until it became a dominant thought (desire) and then demanded (or commanded) His desire into being.

As children of God we have the same creative ability in our minds. Thinking or imagination is the seed of creative power. The ability to imagine is the only mental distinction between a human being and the rest of creation. Apart from this incredible mental ability a human being is no different to other animal species.

By harnessing this ability we can literally create any thing (I mean anything) we desire. Any invention starts in the mind as a simple thought. Every thing that has been created by human being – cars, buildings, shoes, or games- started in one person's imagination. Before any of these things came into reality some one thought about it before putting the thought in a form of a design.

IMAGINATION: THE FAITH FORMULA

Thoughts are things

Imagination is a formation of a mental image. To imagine (or think) is to paint a picture or creating a movie in the mind.

As mentioned earlier a thought is a stimulus – it has the ability to stimulate (or cause) an emotion (or feeling). For example a scary (negative) thought stimulates fear (negative emotion) just as exciting (positive) thoughts stimulates a positive emotion (desire, faith or hope).

To stimulate an emotion a thought has to stick in the mind for some time. The tendency of a thought sticking in the mind is called *mental attention* or *belief.*

That is to say an emotion (negative or positive) is a manifestation (or proof) of what thoughts you believe in. Let me explain

If you are watching a scary movie for example the fact that you feel scared is because you believe what you are watching is real. The excitement you feel by watching a romantic movie is a proof that you believe the actions you are seeing to be real [Or you imagine the actions happening in your real world as you watch].

Therefore belief is equal to mental focus. What your mind chooses to focus turns into a belief. Fear is a negative belief. It is paying attention to a bad thing that you wouldn't like to come true.

On the other hand Faith (desire) is a positive belief. It is paying attention to (believing in) a good thing that you want to come true.

In Hebrews 11:1 Paul said...*faith is a title deed (confirmation of ownership) of the good things we hope for; it is the proof that the exciting things we are hoping for already exists in the spiritual reality. And that we are inevitably going to realise them.*

Fear therefore is a title deed (confirmation of ownership) of the bad things we dread; it is the proof that the awful things we are dreading already exist in the spiritual reality and that we are inevitably going to realise them.

A thought is a fuel for creativity but an emotion is the real creative power. A simple thought does not create anything. But a persistent thought fuels an emotion that creates. For this reason we can also say that *faith is a product of persistent good thought* and *fear is a product of a persistent bad thought.*

PRAYER DYNAMICS

Ask because it has been given

Prayer is another word for creativity. It is the act of commanding those things that exist in the invisible into the visible. It is like printing a hard copy of an electronic file downloaded from the internet. Prayer is pretty much the same as online shopping.

A file (or catalogue) you can see on the internet actually exists-. It was uploaded from a computer to the World Wide Web where it can be accessible to the universe. Any one logged on the respective internet address can actually see and order whatever they like or print as many copies as they like.

Every thought is actually a file on the Spiritual Web. Every imagination is a picture of an object (or situation) that exists in the SW- it can neither be created nor be destroyed. Scientists tell us that every thing is matter- it can exist in different forms or shapes but can neither be created nor destroyed.

God created every thing we human being will ever need well before He created us. Jesus said God our father knows what we need even before we pray. He has made everything available on the Spiritual Web for every one who can desire (order/print) it into a physical equivalent. God has already created all things we may need and kept them in the invisible treasury. We can have them at any time we need them. The mind is the only part of our being that can access the invincible treasury.

I repeat every thing we can think or imagine actually exists. As a matter of fact there are too many other things that we can not even think or imagine at the moment that exists in the SW. The bible says God is able to do amazing things beyond our thinking or imagination[27].

Thinking is visiting a spiritual showroom or browsing spiritual catalogue. Everything you can think about (see by your mind) is available to order for free. God can not allow you to think anything He can not deliver. If you like anything you have seen in the spirit all you need to do is to press an order and it will be delivered.

You do not need to pay anything because we are His children and those things were made for us and for us only! In heaven they do not need what we need here on earth. For example in heaven they do not passports or peace. God is too rich to demand us pay Him for anything. He owns everything including our lives; all things were made by Him and for Him.

FACTS ABOUT PRAYER

1. Every Thing Must Be Prayed For

Every thing we can experience in the physical, as we have discussed, came from the unseen- from the mental (spiritual) world. The bible also says every thing that can be seen was created out of the unseen. In other words every thing that exists in the physical world was created by some one. Yes some were created by God Himself but most of them have been created by men.

God has set up an eternal system whereas nothing can leave heaven unless it has been desired. That is why even God himself when he wanted anything to be delivered in this world he ordered it by faith.

If we lack anything is because we have not prayed for it not because it is not available. Jesus told his poor followers that they were in lack because they had not put their creativity at work[28]. So if we want anything from the spirit that is not under our possession all we need to do is to create it.

Let us revisit a prodigal son story. Every one of the two sons of a wealthy father had a right to posses a certain portion of family fortune. But only one of them enjoyed his right. The younger son enjoyed his wealth because he demanded it. His brother did not enjoy it not because he did not want to, but because he did not demand it. The reason why he did not demand it is because he thought it was his father's responsibility to give it to him.

Many of us are like that big brother. We assume that if really God our wealthy father love us and understands that we need prosperity he must give it to us without asking. The fact is God trusts our desires and respects our freedom of choice. He wants us to grow to the level of making choices that suits our desires. He has created us as his co-workers with the power to will not as robots. He honours and enjoys our desires because, as we have discussed already, our desires are His desires.

We all have the right to enjoy our heavenly father's wealth. But we must demand it. Wealth is attracted to demand no wonder wealthy people – I mean self - made millionaires -are aggressive, demanding and persistent on their desires.

2. Every Prayer Is Answered

Jesus said that every prayer is answered accordingly. Every thing ordered is always delivered[29]. That is why I mentioned above that if you have not received your delivery your order was not received (i.e. you did not order appropriately). If you ordered appropriately your delivery is on its way it will definitely locate you in due time.

When Jesus says ask anything and it is given he means that anything we will ever need was made ready for us before we even think about it[30]. All the angels (divine delivery staff) need from us to deliver is the order.

By saying *'anyone who asks anything'* Jesus meant to say that any one – regardless of religious, racial, mental, or physical distinction - can receive anything from Him. Jesus said if we as parents who love our children and able to provide are delighted to give to our children what they ask us for how far more our heavenly father – who is ever loving and super wealthy- deny us of anything we ask Him?

IT WORKS FOR EVERY ONE

Opportunity dances with those who are already on the dance floor

———————————

H. Jackson Brown Jr.

The law of desire works for every one. It does not matter whether you are a man or a woman, white or black, tall or short. The angels understand just one language- desire; they have no moral standards. After sensing your desire angels do not ask you what for? Angels do have neither ability nor interest to know whether what you are asking for is good for you or not. They are there as your faithful servants- to process and deliver your orders.

Desire is like an automatic door. If you step closer enough for it to feel your movement, it doesn't care whether you are a politician or a doctor, it will swing open for you. It is like pressing an order online. If you click on the appropriate buttons the computer will send your confirmed order. The people that process your order can not know whether you really want what you ordered and for what reason. All they do is to process your order.

The book of Hebrews has a list of the most successful people. They are called men and women of faith because they prospered by faith. They achieved outstanding results through desire.

You do not need to be a Christian or a holy person to have faith, but you cannot be a Christian or a holy person without faith. As a matter of fact faith is the only criterion for holiness. The bible says without faith it is impossible to please God.

Rehab the harlot was not a Christian but she is mentioned along people of faith like Abraham, Isaac and Jacob because she had faith.

A roman soldier was neither a Jew nor a Christian, but he stunned Jesus with his faith. He received healing for his daughter by his faith in Jesus[31].

Quite often Jesus told people 'your faith has healed you'. Or 'receive according to your faith'. Jesus did not heal those people but their demand attracted God's power to heal through Jesus.

God does not respond to pain or need. He responds to demands. He cannot turn down any demand placed before him no matter where that demand comes from.

A legion of demons desired from Jesus to enter the pigs. Jesus did not turn their demand down even if that meant drowning some ones' business in to the sea[32].

Twice divinity satisfied Satan's desire to punish Job[33] .The Devil desired to punish the disciples of Jesus bitterly. Because he demanded it his desire was granted[34]

Divinity also satisfied the demand of an angry crowd for the crucifixion of the innocent Jesus in the place of a criminal.

God does not respond to crying and yelling, he responds to desires. It does not matter how holy we are but if we fail to demand our wealth we will remain in poverty. Failure in desire is desire in failure.

If you believe in what you want to achieve you will certainly achieve it. This explains why people like Hitler and Sadam Hussein were successful even in their evil desires. Being religious or faithful does not make you automatically prosperous. The elder brother to the prodigal son obeyed all of his father's commands yet his wishes were not met because he did not know how to make his wishes come true.

WHY GOD GRANTS EVEN 'BAD' DESIRES

People take different roads seeking fulfilment and happiness. Just because they're not on your road doesn't mean they've gotten lost.

H. Jackson Brown, Jr.

I know many of you are asking, "If God is truly a loving father why should he grant evil desires or create evil things in the first place?" I think this is a very good question as well as a complex one. Because of its complexity it demands thorough discussion – a discussion that I endeavour to have at a later time in a separate book. But in short let me bring into your attention these facts

First everything God has created is good for the world. But good is a relative word; it stands for satisfaction of a need, suit one's taste or size. Since we differ in needs, tastes and size we differ in what is good. Good for me is not necessarily good for every one. For example coke is my wife's best drink but I like passion juice. Although we all need a drink we differ in what satisfies our drink needs. Again I and my son Adili both like watching football but we support different teams. Both Adili and I like *Nike* shoes but we wear different sizes.

Every thing that fits our needs is good for us. The only way we know that it is good for us it is because it make us feel good – we love it; we desire it. And anything that does not fit our need is the wrong thing for us. The reason why it is wrong for us is because it causes us pain; we hate it.

But because we hate something it is wrong to think that that thing shouldn't have been created in the first place why? Because it is the right thing for somebody else.

At times one thing can be good to day and bad the other day. This is because things do change. Somebody said nothing is permanent except change. Sometimes things change or we (our needs, tastes and sizes) change .For example fresh milk can be good to day but the same milk might be yoghurt by the beginning of next week. In this case the thing- the milk- has changed. Fresh milk can be perfect for breakfast but fresh milk might not be good for lunch because I might prefer yoghurt instead. In this case my need has changed. So the same thing might be good at one time and bad at another time.

Put it in other words every thing has the 'bad' side and the 'good' side. Nothing is 100% good or 100% bad. That is why two people might experience the same thing but feel differently. Let me give you another simple example

I support Arsenal Football Club but my son Adili supports Manchester United. If Arsenal and Manchester United were to play against each other on a cup final one of us is set for disappointment. A win to either of the team means a defeat to the other. Same score but different meaning and reaction from both of us.

Angels have no intelligence to know whether what we have ordered is good for us or not. We are the ones who should know whether what we ordered is good for us or not before we press the order. The sad fact is that many of us make wrong choices. I mean we order wrong things unknowingly. In other words many people do not know how to pray.

So instead of being annoyed by the presence of 'bad' things we need to appreciate God's goodness of giving us the luxury of choice to suit our desires at all times. Instead of blaming the abundance of options and variety we should learn how to make the right choices for ourselves.

HOW DO PEOPLE ASK FOR WRONG THINGS?

Prayer is what dominates the mind. The principle that says we always get what we pray for actually means we always get what dominates our minds not what we want or profess. So make sure what dominates your mind is what you want.

Paul said the Spirit helps us to pray appropriately because we do not know how to pray. The fact is not that we do not know what to pray but how to pray. Many do not believe that every prayer is answered because from their understanding many of their 'prayers' have not been answered. But, as you will understand later, they have either prayed for a wrong thing or have not prayed at all. Let us see how cans this happen.

I think you know by now that faith is the prayer language. The angels who process our prayers being spirits do not understand any other language other than the language of emotional feelings. Paul says the spirit uses groaning – a strong desire to give birth to something long awaited and precious - when praying for us not words.

As we discussed there are two types of belief; a positive belief (faith) and a negative belief (fear). But a belief is a product of mental focus – a thought that sticks into our minds long enough to produce a feeling. When these feelings are strong enough they are picked by angels as orders or prayers. The angels then translate the feelings into the spiritual equivalent of what caused the feeling (the stimulus). And in due cause the angels dispatch it back to the person who produced the feeling (the person who believed) as the physical equivalent.

In practical terms we pray by mental pictures (thoughts) - not by words. In the spirit realm mental focus means love. The angels know what you want by looking at what is dominant in your mind. Putting it in other words what populates your mind (not your mouth) is your prayer. If you say one thing and believe the other what you are going to receive is what you believe. If you want one thing but believe the other what you are going to get is what you believe – full stop!

Many people want one thing but actually believe (pray) exactly the opposite. This is because their mind is filled with what they do not want to happen. Their mind is so obsessed with what they do not want to happen to the extent that they actually believe (fear) it.

Let us say you have received bad news from your doctor that you have terminal cancer and that you have few days to live. How you feel after the news says a lot about whether you believe the doctor or not. If you feel great (faith) it means you do not believe the doctor. To the contrary you believe something good (healing) is about to happen to you. But if you feel devastated with fear it means you believe the doctor and that death is imminent. As long as your mind is focusing on death, as far as the angels are concerned, you are asking for death.

Even if you are confessing healing at the top of your voice, as long as you are still feeling the fear, what you are actually asking for is what causes the fear – death. And unless you change your mental focus to something you really want – healing- you are bonded to get more of what you do not want.

Remember I said the angels do not understand whether the feeling is negative or positive. Angels are not all-knowing-creatures; they can not distinguish between fear and faith. All they pick is a feeling – a belief. The only person who can distinguish between the two is you – a believer. And this, to repeat what I said in the previous chapters, has been done purposely to help us know what kind of thing we are actually praying for. Feeling has been designed to let us know whether what we are asking for is good for us or not. And if not to cancel our prayer before it is too late.

In Romans chapter ten verse nine and ten Paul says to be saved from danger your confession and belief must be in harmony. If you say you will live but you believe in your heart (and fear in your face confirms) that you are going to die you are on your way to the grave.

Melvin D. Saunders said … *We get what we are thinking about whether we want it or not. Our intentional thought chooses the direction. The Universe doesn't recognize whether the thought is positive or negative, the Universe does recognize that we are focusing on it and magnetizes it to us. This Law of Attraction works even in our ignorance of it.*

Few years ago my wife fell terribly ill. And she remained in a critical condition for sometime. During that time I was gripped with fear of me loosing my wife and my two young children loosing their mother in a foreign land. It was a very difficult time physically, financially and emotionally.

On one particular day I was overcome by devastating fear and grief. In the midst of my grief I heard a small, but calm refreshing voice inside of me telling me that my wife will not die. I was assured that my wife and I still have an assignment on earth that will take many years to accomplish. Immediately my focus shifted from death to life. And that simple shift of thought brought back life and energy into my bones. I felt strong and vibrant and my tears dried instantly.

When I went back to the hospital my wife's condition was even worse. As I was tempted to focus on death again, that voice kept on playing in my spirit "my wife will not die; we still have many years of life and mission together" immediately   my faith and strength came back. Few days later the doctor broke potentially bad news. They told me that my wife's condition was seriously terminal and that she literally had few days to live. Understanding what was at stake doctors had counsellors handy to help me coupe with the news in case I break down.

To their amazement I was extremely calm. The little voice of faith that never stopped buzzing in my heart kept me strong. Literally I did not believe what the doctors were saying. Instead I believed that little voice within me. Before they knew it I opened my mouth and said exactly what that voice was saying in me "my wife is not going to die but live; we still have many years of life and mission together".

The doctors thought I did not understand what they said. So they kept on repeating the same thing with greater emphasis. Again I made them understand that I clearly understood what they were saying and that they should also understand what I was saying. They finally left me alone thinking I was out of my mind already.

That night when I went back home I had to fight the faith battle of my life. It was quite a challenge to stop tears from wetting my bed as I tried to contemplate life without my lovely wife. I tried to think how I could cope with raising small kids on my own in England. As I thought that I felt weak and lifeless. But immediately that little voice came up into my mind and spirit but this time with colourful motion pictures. I could vividly imagine me and my healthy wife travelling around the world with our grown up children as we fulfil our destiny. As I held these thoughts in my mind I felt extremely good and strong.

The next morning something amazing happened. My wife who could not speak, could not open her eyes, could not respond to any medication or feeding was up walking, eating and responding to treatment. To cut the long story short the next day –literally the day doctors said she will probably die – my wife was out of hospital. To day nine years latter my wife and our (now three) children are still alive and full of energy. The book you are now reading is part of that life mission we are still fulfilling together.

This is what I mean by faith. Holding in your heart and mind a vivid picture of what you want to happen so tightly that it produces a nice strong feeling as if what you want has already happened. By doing that, not only that you will feel good instantly, you will literally bring what you want into reality.

Many Christians think faith is to deny the reality by professing the opposite of a negative reality. If one is sick for example they say *"I am not sick"*. Immediately after finishing the confession the pain resumes and often times with enhanced intensity. Empty confessions of this nature serve no greater good other than lying to oneself and making the situation worse. The very reason that one still fearful after confession proves that one still believes in exactly the opposite. But more importantly there is something wrong with the wording of the confession itself.

'I am not sick' makes being sick the backbone of the confession. By saying *'I am not sick'* one has to think of being sick many times over before thinking of being well. As the *being sick* picture flashes in ones mind many times over it eventually sticks in the mind and believed.

What is required is to accept the present reality but focus on your desired future. Accept what has happened but delete the pictures of the past and fill your mind, soul and body with the pictures of what you want to happen now and into the future.

This is what I did. I did not deny the medical fact that my wife was seriously ill. But I did not accept doctor's prognosis that my wife is going to die that soon. I knew one day she, like every other human being, will surely die. But I believed she still have many years and a destiny to live for - not few days. I did not struggle with the past or present problem; instead I confronted my favourite future with a mind and mouth littered with images and words that depicts my desire.

We have a traditional saying that goes like this; *'if you want to kill a monkey don't look at its face'.*

The traditional meaning behind the saying is that if you want to kill a monkey while gazing at its face the chances are that you will feel sorry for it and change your mind. But the meaning I want you to get is this- if you want to solve your problem do not confront it. I mean don't wrestle with your problem instead confront your solution.

I know this may shock some of you but the wisdom behind this principle is that to wrestle with a problem you must face it- you must keep it in mind. And by doing so you are causing your mind to believe it .That is why when one wrestles with a problem one feels terribly fearful. This sort of condition diminishes one's ability to deal with the problem and therefore make the problem more stubborn.

But confronting a solution means putting desired solution under mental spotlight. It is populating the mind with an assimilated version of what you really want to come true. This is what we have been talking about- faith.

A positive sign (+) has two strokes crossing each other; a horizontal stroke and a vertical stroke. A negative sign (-) is one stroke short (a vertical stroke) from making it a positive sign. In real life this signifies that any negative entity is nothing but an absence or short of an important component of perfection. For example darkness is nothing but the absence of light. Fear is the absence of faith; illness is the absence of wellness; hatred is the absence of love and poverty is lack of prosperity.

The best way to turn a negative entity into a positive one is to restore the missing component. For example to solve a darkness problem one needs to restore light. And to restore light one must think about the source of light. If you want to eradicate poverty don't fight it; instead focus on prosperity. The best way to fight illiteracy is to focus on literacy. The perfect way to combat hatred is to turn our minds away from it and think about love.

So be careful what you are focusing at for surely, as Napoleon Hill once said, *whatever the mind can conceive and believe, it can achieve.*

Abraham Lincoln also said *"You can have anything you want if you want it badly enough. You can be anything you want to be, do anything you set out to accomplish if you hold to that desire with singleness of purpose".*

HOW TO KINDLE YOUR DESIRE

I'm very determined and stubborn. There's a desire in me that makes me want to do more and more, and to do it right. Each one of us has a fire in our heart for something. It's our goal in life to find it and to keep it.

_____

Mary Lou Retton

Desire has got life. Like any living thing it can be consciously conceived, born, grown and killed. Desire is like fire that warms and fuels our life. Like any fire it can be deliberately started, sustained, and distinguished.

To keep the desire burning we must first understand the nature of desire; we must know how it can be started, sustained, and distinguished.

To start a fire one must have two things; an ignition (source of heat like a spark) and fuel (something that can catch fire when ignited like petrol). An ignition and fuel on their own can not cause fire. There has to be contact between them – there must be an agent to put the two together; something like a person or wind.

The strength of the fire is determined by the strength (quality and quantity) of both the ignition and fuel. For example a fire in the oil refinery is stronger than the fire in a small paper bin. So one can grow, sustain or distinguish the fire by regulating the strength of either of them or both. I mean one can grow the fire by increasing (or spreading) the ignition, injecting more fuel or both. To reduce the fire strength one can reduce the strength of the ignition, the fuel or both. And to put off the fire completely one can turn off the ignition, cut off the fuel or both.

To have a feeling one must have two things; a *thought* and *meaning* . A thought is like fuel and meaning is like an ignition.

As you might have known by now a thought is a mental image of a present (physical) or past/future (spiritual) reality. It is an image in the mind that represents something happening in the now, here in the natural or something that happened sometime in the past or it is anticipated to happen in the unseen (supernatural) future world.

Meaning stands for a thinker's association of a thought with a certain importance or contribution; it is linking a thought with either pain or pleasure. The process of attaching meaning to a thought is called *understanding*.

Just as fuel can not catch fire on its own without an ignition, a thought can not stimulate any feeling without attaching any meaning to it. I mean an image has no power to stimulate fear or hope without attaching a fearful (painful) or hopeful (pleasurable) meaning to it. That is to say the type (negative or positive) and strength (weak or intense) of a feeling depends pretty much on both the thought and more importantly the corresponding meaning.

For example if one sees (or thinks of) a cobra how one feels about it (fearful or otherwise) is subject to how one understands cobra. For most of us cobra is a snake blessed with lethal venom that can kill human beings instantly. We also understand that death is painful and takes away our life that we dearly treasure. Most of us associate cobra with a bad thing- death. So whenever we see or think of a cobra we feel bad about it; we feel terror. But the same cobra thought will not evoke a bad feeling to a person (a small child for example) who do not understand cobra like the most of us. This explains why two people might see or think about the same thing but react differently.

One thing can mean a blessing to one person but the same thing can mean entirely something else to the other. For instance my family name (Maturlu) symbolically means a hardworking ethic in my mother tongue. But in a chagga vernacular (my wife's mother tongue) the word maturlu actually stands for something embarrassing. You can imagine how challenging it was to introduce yourself to your in-laws who traditionally address men by their family names.

The letters spelled C-A-N-C-E-R on a doctor's report have no power what so ever to make one freeze with fear. But the meaning behind the letters does. What makes one go crazy to the extent of committing suicide is not the negative sign before [or two letters (DR) after] a huge number in a bank statement ; but what that number mean to one's business and life in general. If one shifts the focus from the depressing thought (the unhealthy financial statement) to something desirable; if one changes the meaning of the financial statement (for example stop linking a bad financial state with unbearable desperate life situation); or if one does both it will definitely make a huge positive change to one's feeling.

So the magic secret of desire is to choose what you want, make a bright, clear, gigantic near-real image of it and make it stick in your mind and soul for as long as possible. If you do this you will be fine - guaranteed!

Again Napoleon Hill said, *"The starting point of all achievement is desire. Keep this constantly in mind. Weak desires bring weak results, just as a small amount of fire makes a small amount of heat"*.

THE ANATOMY OF FOCUS

A person who aims at nothing is sure to hit it.

Unknown Author

Certain conditions favour the sustenance or spread of fire; conditions such as the nature of fuel or ignition, air, wind, temperature and drought. Like wise there are certain conditions that make thoughts stick quickly and longer into our minds and there fore affect the intensity of our feelings. I mean there are certain factors that affect the polarity and the intensity of our focus. It is imperative to study these factors because the polarity (negativity or positivity) of our focus tells us whether we are taking the right direction or not. And the intensity of our focus tells us how fast we are travelling. A strong negative feeling tells us we are moving towards the wrong direction very fast and vice versa

Basically there are five factors that affect our focus. To make it easier to remember I have spelled these five factors as F-O-C-U-S. They are Ferocity, Occupation, Clarity, Uniqueness and Sensitivity.

Ferocity
By ferocity I mean how strong the thought is. The ferocity of a thought is determined by type and size. For example big screen coloured motion pictures with a loud sound have stronger impact in our minds than a small screen black and white still pictures.

Live real life scenarios are more ferocious in our minds than recorded or fictional equivalents. For this reason they catch our attention quickly and stimulate a long lasting feeling (belief).

Pictures are more effective compared to words. A word is a description of a certain reality. But a picture is a closer representation of a reality if not a reality itself. For example the word 'cow' is a short description of an animal. Unless one has seen a cow before it will require more words (and perhaps more than words) to get the person understand the cow. But if one sees the picture of a cow even if it is for the first time one gets closer to a real cow than hearing thousand words about a cow.

So to be understood better and remembered quickly words must be converted into pictures. After all written words by themselves are just pictures of letters arranged in a certain shape.

Occupation

Occupation stands for the duration of a thought occupies the mind; how long or how often the thought flashes in our minds determines it's sticking ability. The longer the thought stays in the mind the more it sticks. For example if you keep a thought for a long time it will eventually produce a strong feeling. Even if a thought flashes just for few seconds but flashes too often it will equally produce a stronger feeling. This is because every time a thought flashes produces sparks of belief in the mind. These small beliefs continue to accumulate until a stronger belief is formed.

This explains why big businesses pay millions of pounds for a 30 second tv/radio commercial that runs for months. The marketing people know that if you see these cleverly crafted ads more often you will eventually buy the products.

Clarity

It has been said *'clarity is power'*. Clarity of a thought produces a stronger belief. By clarity I mean the quality of a mental image that determines the number of specific details the mind can gather from the image; the clearer the thought the stronger the belief. A moving image in a big high definition screen television produces a stronger and long lasting effect in the mind than the images on a mini analogue television screen. A clear sound has a greater impact on our feeling compared to a dull one.

Uniqueness

Uniqueness is in the contrast of a thought. Uniqueness catches our imagination better than uniformity or conformity; different ideas no matter how bizarre they might be, arouses our curiosity hence stealing our focus. It is easier to see a small white spot on a black background than to see a big dark blue one. A unique thought stimulates stronger faith because it catches our attention better. That is why anything new (new partner or a new house) is more exciting even if it is not necessarily better than the old one.

I think this also explains why bad things generate stronger interest than the good ones. The reason why good things make us feel good in the first place is because they are in harmony with our being; they are part of our genetic makeup. Remember we are god's children. And goodness (love, peace and prosperity) is our father's nature. To the contrary bad things are not part of our being; bad things are aliens to our humanity that is why our minds treat them as such.

Sensitivity
Sensitive things draw our attention. In fact one way you can know how important the issue is to a person is the level of attention is being devoted to the issue. In the spiritual world love is equal to attention and attention is equal to love. Angels know that the thing that draws one's attention the most is the one's dearest.

There are two things that motivate our actions - pain and pleasure. Primarily our actions are motivated by an attempt to gain (move towards) pleasure or avoid (manage) pain. Unfortunately for the reasons discussed earlier ordinary people pay much attention to the issues that are perceived to have the greatest potential to inflict intense pain. For example most people want to be rich because they do not want to be poor. Because the attention is on a painful thing (poverty) many people wonder why they end up having the very dreadful thing. Even when they get lucky enough and accumulate much wealth in the process these people never feel wealthy. They constantly feel poor because their focus is on poverty not on wealth.

In the light of what we have learnt so far the best way to avoid or manage pain (which is essentially the absence of pleasure) is to pay much attention to the things that have the greatest potential to inject much pleasure.

While in the wilderness the Israelites were succumbed by terrible disaster. Many people died as a result of being bitten by poisonous snakes. After a bitter cry God instructed Moses their leader to make a bronze snake and hang it on a flagpole. *"Whoever is bitten and looks at it"*, God instructed, *"will live"*. So Moses made a snake of fiery copper and put it on top of a flagpole. Anyone bitten by a snake who then looked at the copper snake lived[35].

This scenario pitimises the power of focus by simulation. Focusing on a dead snake took ones eyes away from a live poisonous snake. Apart from neutralising the venom, the action also prevented even further biting. An attempt to sort the snake out kept the live snake in sight and made its venom more effective.

Focusing on the problem keeps the problem alive to kill you. What kills therefore is not the problem but the focus on the problem. What ever you focus on comes to you. If you focus on failure, failure will come to you. If you focus on your desire, your desire will come into a reality.

I use this power to my advantage in my everyday life. For example I can get parking spaces at any location of my choosing at any time. What I normally do is vividly imagine any parking space I want before I start my journey. By the time I get there the very parking space or the adjacent one will be available for me. Some times I had to wait for few minutes before the parking space can be available.

At one point I wanted to go to the bank during lunch time. I had visited this local branch many times before so I knew it was more than likely I would spend a long time on a queue. Since I wasn't ready for a delay I decided to put my faith to the test. Because I wanted to be in front of the queue I clearly imagined I was in front of the queue and spent just few minutes before being served. When I arrived at the bank   there were only two people in front of me. The guy that was in front of the queue moved to the vacant teller to be served just as I was settling down. And suddenly the lady that was in front of me seemed unsettled. Just before she was about to be served she quickly excused herself as if she had an emergency to attend. Surprisingly she stepped back just a couple of steps and joined the queue behind me. She literally allowed me to be served next without saying a word!

DESIRE PRACTISE

"I believe that you tend to create your own blessings. You have to prepare yourself so that when opportunity comes, you're ready."

_____

Oprah Winfrey

The aim of this exercise is to produce maximum desire for what we want to happen. To achieve our aim we must hook our mind to what we want to happen. We must saturate our mind with a simulated version of what we want to happen. And this is how to do it

A. Describe Your Desire

It is the man's duty to set up the plan, but is God's duty to fulfil it - King Solomon[36]

Decide and describe exactly what you want. Your description must be precise and clear.

If you want a car for example you have to have these details. Car make, model, type (body shape), fuel type (petrol/diesel), mileage (or age), colour, engine size, and gear box transmission. If you like your car to have extras like stereo, GPS, electrics or alloy wheels make sure you include them in your description.

At this stage the most important thing is to make sure you know what you really want. Do not let prices or the value of the car influence your choice in a negative way. Remember the divine store is able to deliver anything and everything you will ever want. All the angels need from you is your order and the rest is up to them. They know the best way to make your dream happen. I repeat, at this stage (and indeed at any stage) never allow your current financial situation to limit your desire. Never even bother yourself thinking when your desire will materialise. Because having received your order the angels will choose the cheapest, the most enjoyable and the quickest way possible to make it happen.

In my judgement attaching time limit to your desire is to attach unnecessary potential destruction. This is because you are likely to be tempted to keep an eye on time as well.

People say 'look where you are going'. But I say look where you want to go. Because in the spirit realm what your mind sees is what you get. So make sure your mind sees what you want to get. Know exactly what you want; be specific; be definite.

Napoleon Hill once said *"The battle is all over except the "shouting" when one knows what is wanted and has made up his mind to get it, whatever the price may be"*.

B. Write down Your Vision

…Write what you see. Write it out in big block letters so that it can be read on the run[37].

Vision is a written (or paper form of a) desire. It is has been established that less than 5% of us have visions. And less than 1% of us have taken time to write down our visions.

A research conducted many years ago found that only 3% of 1953 Yale University graduates had written down their financial goals. Surprisingly twenty years later the 3% had more income than a combined income of the 97% of the graduates who had no written visions. Could this be one of the reasons why so few people are living their dream life?

Writing your vision is a crucial creative process. Even God our father writes His visions. He wrote down the law on the tablets for His people by His own finger before giving it to their leader Moses[38].

Why is it important to write down your vision? In my opinion there are a couple of reasons. First the process of writing down your vision forces your mind to focus on your desire. Also writing down your goal gives you the point of reference that makes it easy to visualise and enact.

How to write your desire

I suggest your vision to be written in a '4P' format.

a. Personal
Write your vision in a 'first person singular' form. For example if your desire is to own a house your vision may look like this; *I own a house*

b. Present
Your vision has to be written in a present tense. Describe it as if it is happening now or it has happened already. By doing this you create a reality impression in your mind and therefore activate a positive feeling. For example if your desire is to move into your own house your vision may look like this; *I am living in my own house*

c. Positive
To reduce resistance and maximise the flow of a positive feeling a vision must be written in a positive way. Do not include any negative word in your description. For example if your desire is to be well your vision may look like this; *I am well*. Instead of *I am not sick*

d. Precise
As discussed earlier your vision has to be written with precision and clarity. For example if your desire is to own a car your vision may read like this;

I own a brand new an automatic diesel silver BMW X6 with Twin Turbo Auto tiptronic, profesional SatNav, Media pack Dynamic Pack, Blue Tooth telephone Black leather memory heated sports seats, alloys with run flat tyres. Head up display showing sat nav, fitted with a track star, rear parking camera, front and rear parking sensors, USB for MP3 player, internet, alloy running boards, electric folding mirrors and auto dimming mirror, digital radio, and multi cd.

If you can get a clear coloured (still) picture of what you want is even better. If you need a car for example you can get a nice poster, catalogue or brochure from the nearest dealer. You can also download pictures from the internet.

Stick your vision   where ever you can frequently and clearly see. I normally stick my vision on my bed, on my bedroom door, on the wad rob, in front of my shaving mirror and on my laptop screen saver. I actually carry one with me on the wallet and stick one in the car. I also make a hard copy folder for it. You can decorate your lap top and or your desk top computer screens with your vision.

In an experimental exercise to boost their penalty taking performance basket ball players were divided in to three groups. Players in group one were asked to take field practise for two weeks. The players in group two were asked to do nothing for two weeks and the last group were asked to take mental practise. (i.e to imagine that they are practising) for two weeks. After two weeks the performance of the players in group one increased by 2% while that of group two dropped by 2%. Surprisingly the performance of players in group three (those who practised by imagination) improved their performance by 3.5%

You can do the same to improve your efficiency. Every day set aside few minutes - first thing in the morning and last thing before falling asleep- to clearly, soundly and intensely affirm your vision. As you do this clearly imagine yourself actually enjoying your desire. Keep doing this until you experience an exciting feeling inside you.

C. Simulate your Desire

J.G. Gallimore once said; *Image creates desire. You will want what you imagine.* So simulation involves imitation or enactment of a desire; it is the process of pretending, acting or feigning your desire. The essence of simulation is to create a real impression of your desire in order to generate maximum positive feeling. Simulation is a rehearsal; a practise session that prepares our mind to receive, manage and enjoy what we desire. It includes doing anything that will cause your mind to feel the reality of what you desire. This may include practices such as scouting.

Scouting

Scouting is a search made for the purpose of collecting useful information about your desire. It is a fact finding mission for your desire. It involves going into the field to conduct examination or survey of a region, product, person or situation you want to realise.

A scouting mission is one of the most effective focus practises. If you want to accelerate the reality process of your physically visible desire go and experience it as you feel the excitement. If you desire a car for example arrange a test drive. If you have passion to become a surgeon you can go to your local hospital and shake hands with one of your favourite surgeons. If you desire a certain property arrange a visit if possible and have some pictures of it. You can do the same if you desire to be in a relationship with a certain person or you want to emulate your hero's success.

Before taking the Promised Land God instructed Moses to send twelve spies to scout the land. Many times they heard Mosses telling them how good the land was. But before they could be motivated to possess it God wanted them to have a taste of the land by themselves. As he sent them for a scouting mission Moses said

Go up through the Negev and then into the hill country. Look the land over, see what it is like. Assess the people: Are they strong or weak? Are there few or many? Observe the land: Is it pleasant or harsh? Describe the towns where they live: Are they open camps or fortified with walls? And the soil: Is it fertile or barren? Are there forests? And try to bring back a sample of the produce that grows there--this is the season for the first ripe grapes."[39]

God told Joshua *'every place that the sole of your foot shall tread upon, that have I given unto you.....'*[40]

We cannot possess the city we have not scouted. God will release to us what we desire but only when we dare to put our feet to tread on.

If it is impossible to arrange a scouting mission paint a picture of your desire or make a simulated version. Be creative and curious; just do anything that brings you closer to the reality of your desire. Practise having it and see it in your mind as if it has happened.

Nelson Mandela had a life long desire to become the first black president of a democratic South Africa. In a movie (Sarafina) Nelson Mandela is depicted practising acceptance speech while still in prison. It is not surprising therefore Mandela was released from prison and realised his desire few days after the movie was released.

Perhaps one of the most inspiring stories that illustrate the power of desire simulation is that of Jacob. Laban – Jacob's father in law - agreed to give Jacob all the young streaked or spotted or speckle animals born in his flock as his wages .To make all the young animals streaked or spotted or speckle Jacob got fresh branches from poplar, almond, and plane trees and peeled the bark, leaving white stripes on them. He stuck the peeled branches in front of the watering troughs where the flocks came to drink. When the flocks were in heat, they came to drink and mated in front of the streaked branches. Then they gave birth to young that were streaked or spotted or speckled[41].

My Scouting Mission

A while ago I had a desire for television studio equipments. As you probably know television equipments are very expensive and at the time I did not have enough money for that purpose. Again I decided to stretch my faith. I got colourful pictures of the equipments I wanted and plastered them in front of my desk. Every day I would see them and feel them as already under my possession.

To make it even more sensational I arranged a visit to one of the mega churches in London that owned the equipments I desired. Between program intervals I went around the stage curiously gazing and touching the cameras, tripods and mixers. I did that several times until I felt a worm exciting feeling inside of me.

On my return I did set aside three days of believing practice. These were three days of visualising and affirming my desire. It was a wonderful time to practise (in my mind) receiving and owning the equipments. During that time I also used my mouth to affirm my desire.

Literally, few months after this believing exercise I bought all the equipments I desired. And I got a half of them without paying a penny upfront! What astonished me even more is finding out one of the studio equipments I bought -a brand new professional apple computer- was manufactured on the last day of my believing practise!

I came to realise the manufacture date as I was trying to get help with software installation. The on-line technician wanted a serial number for my computer that happened to be alongside the manufacture date. The date instantly rang a bell because it was still fresh in my mind.

Diligence is the mother of success. But believing is the only diligent work that is required to achieve anything you want. Paul said that physical training is good, but training for the sake of believing is much better; promising benefits in this life and in the life to come.[42]

I know some of you may find simulation a tiring or crazy exercise. But believe me it is effective, none tiring and incredibly fun. Believing is more exhilarating than any drug you can ever find. It is impossible to feel down when you are thinking something you really love. The fact that practising your desire literally turns your desires into a reality without any negative side effect in your life makes it worth trying.

Professional athletes know that practise is the mother of perfection. They put many efforts in physical training but more importantly they train their minds.

Recently Serena Williams -the current number one female tennis player - won the 2008 US open. At a press conference she said the following in relation to her extraordinary success.

I have been working so hard all year. Sometimes I wake up at like six in the morning to go practise and it was too dark, I have to wait until it gets light. No one really knows the work that an athlete puts in. you know it's worth it. Then I felt like Gosh, I've been working the hardest. I should win.

Remember whatever the mind constantly sees conceives. And whatever the mind conceives achieves. So if you want to make your dream come true you must remember to practise, practise, and practise.

THE POWER OF PATIENCE

All things come to him who waits provided he knows what he is waiting for.

Woodrow T. Wilson

Patience is the ability to suppress restlessness or annoyance when confronted with delay. It is the willingness to remain calm, collected and upbeat when we encounter setbacks or when our desires take longer to materialise.

The reason why I am bringing up the issue of patience is because most desires take time to materialise. Having received your order angels endeavour to process and deliver it as soon as it practically possible. I say as soon as it is practically possible because there are certain practicalities that must be in place before the desire can be delivered.

First all desires are in a spiritual form. Before they can be delivered in the physical world they must be transformed in to a physical format. The process of transforming the desires into a physical reality takes time. The transformation time varies with the type of the desire. Some desires take longer than others.

All physical things take time to prepare. Each thing has to be prepared in a certain way according to its original divine design. If it is delivered prematurely it won't be good enough. That is why angels can not be pushed to deliver our order before its due time.

Patience is the key character of God our father. Even He is bonded with time when it comes to issues of this planet earth. The bible tells us that despite having all He needed to finish His world project, it took Him six heavenly days to get it done. Jesus Christ had to wait for thirty years to accomplish his three and a half year mission. Abraham had to wait for twenty four years to see Isaac his son of promise.

There is no such thing as a miracle when it comes to creative process. All 'miracles' are created by using certain principles that are uncommon to ordinary people but can be learnt and practised in a common way. So patience plays a key role in any creative process. I had to wait for a couple of weeks for my television studio equipment because they had to be processed to my specifications. All tailor made desires are made to order. And if what you desire is of any value, it is worth waiting for.

Another reason is that the angels must make sure that we are ready for the desire. Even if what we desire is ready the angels might not deliver the desire if we are not ready for it. So patience prepares us to enjoy and keep what we desire. The energy we need to attain our desire is the same energy we will need to retain it.

God is a prudent God. He wants us to enjoy and manage well what we demand. He values both us as well as what we desire because He is the creator of both. He does not want to give us something that will destroy us or abuse it due to poor management. So before He can allow us to possess anything He must make sure we can manage it well.

Let us say for example you believe God for a baby. God will never give you a baby unless you are physically, psychologically and financially ready. If He does He is likely to destroy both you and the baby.

This applies to all things including material wealth. God will never release wealth unless we are prepared to manage it well.

God has no problem releasing anything to us, but He want to make sure we are prepared to receive and hold it before releasing it. I think you will agree with me that wealth has much to do with how much is retained rather than how much is attained. Most of us have no problem receiving money. But wealthy people - who happen to be very few - have a very strong money retaining capacity.

God created all things for us human beings to enjoy and manage. Because He created them for us in the first place there is no way He can deny us from possessing them. But He must train and prepare us for the same.

The desire acts as a motivation or as a fuel to undergo the necessary preparatory training to receive and manage what we desire. Patience therefore is a necessary ingredient that prepares us to receive and manage what we desire.

Maturity (or righteousness) is the right character or management skills. Every thing in this world has got a proper way to handle it. That is why we do have different ways of receiving things from God. The way you received your car for example is quite different from the way you will receive your job.

The pressure and the trouble we undergo in asking, knocking and seeking produces the right character for what we are demanding for.

If your order is taking longer do not worry. The delay means your desire is valuable. A delay is not a denial so keep on asking, keep on seeking and knocking until you receive it.

B. C. Forbes once said '*History has demonstrated that the most notable winners usually encountered heartbreaking obstacles before they triumphed. They won because they refused to become discouraged by their defeats*'.

If you are seeking for something do not give up until you find it. If you can desire it you can definitely have it; what we need to do is to keep on seeking. Someone said, *when you are wrestling a gorilla you do not rest when you are tired, you rest when the gorilla is tired*. If you have tried several times without success do not be discouraged. Know that you are not doing the right thing. You haven't discovered the perfect formula. Keep on working on your project. Change your method and seek new ideas.

Thomas Alva Edison the American inventor failed more than 10,000 times before getting the result he wanted. When he was asked how he felt that he failed all those times he said '*I have not failed once. I have just found 10,000 ways that won't work.*

Charlie Dexter wrote

> *Unfortunately, we are trying to live our fast paced lifestyle in what is naturally a slow paced world. (But) people, who*

patiently toil towards worthwhile dreams and goals, building strong character while overcoming adversity and challenge, grow the strong internal foundation to handle success, while get-rich- quickers and lottery winners usually are unable to sustain unearned sudden wealth. A caterpillar is doomed to a life on the ground if it is freed from its struggle inside a cocoon prematurely. The struggle in the cocoon is what gives the future butterfly the wing power to fly, just as tension against muscles as we exercise strengthen our muscles, while muscles left alone will soon atrophy. My problem with exercise is not getting instantly stronger after each work out! I pray for more patience every day and I pray to get it right now!

PRIZE FUELS PATIENCE

The brick walls are there for a reason: they let us prove how badly we want things

———————————

Dr. Randy Pausch

An obstacle -in a form of a set back, cost or hard work- is like a door lock. A lock is designed to deny access to those who don't have the key. An obstacle is designed to discourage those who do not have a desire. Simply put the key to an obstacle is handed to a person who can prove a strong desire for the reward of overcoming an obstacle.

Patience is a proof of a desire. You prove how badly you want something by how long are you willing to wait for it.

But patience is fuelled by the reward. What gives you the strength to wait is what that you are waiting for means to you.

The value of a key is determined by the value of what is behind the lock. The strength of a winning motivation is in the value of the prize. Focusing on a prize instead of a price is a key to overcoming any obstacle. That is why before taking up the challenge to compete athletes do check the prizes first.

Paul was ready to damp every thing for the sake of an ultimate prize of enjoying sound living by acting on the teachings of Christ.

I once thought all these things were so very important, but now I consider them worthless because of what Christ has done. Yes, everything else is worthless when compared with the priceless gain of knowing [the teaching of] Christ Jesus my Lord. I have discarded everything else, counting it all as garbage, so that I may [keep the knowledge of the secret of sound living as taught by] Christ[43] .

David was motivated to fight Goliath by the prize that was on offer for defeating the giant. He put his life on the line because he wanted to be the King, become extremely rich and marry King Saul's beautiful daughter[44]. Even Samson the giant needed motivation from a beautiful woman before he could fight[45].

Great prize motivates great faith. The author of the book of Hebrews said *'but without faith it is impossible to please him; for he that cometh to God must believe that he is, and that **he is a rewarder of them that diligently seek him**.*[46]

Even Peter and his fellow disciples wanted to know the prize of following Jesus before they could continue pledging their support for His ministry. And Jesus replied,

"I assure you that when I, the Son of Man, sit upon my glorious throne in the Kingdom, you who have been my followers will also sit on twelve thrones, judging the twelve tribes of Israel. And everyone who has given up houses or brothers or sisters or father or mother or children or property, for my sake, will receive a hundred times as much in return here on earth plus eternal life.[47]

The reason why Jesus endured the pain of the cross is because of the prize He was promised to get. He knew He would be crowned the king of kings and the lord of lords. He had an eye on the prize of having the name above all names. Paul said

*… let us run with patience the race that is set before us by taking the example of Jesus the author and finisher of our faith; who **for the joy that was set before him** endured the cross, despising the shame, and is seated at the right hand of the throne of God*[48].

So always remember to keep an eye on the prize; always remember what are you fighting for and why!

THE ART OF PLANNING

He who fails to plan, plans to fail

———————————

Unknown source

Planning is making deliberate arrangement for the future. It involves deciding what you want to happen, when you want it to happen and make necessary preparations. As we have discovered having your wishes for the future is never good enough to make those wishes come to pass.

The only reason why we must plan ahead of time is because nothing happens without been prepared. I repeat every thing must be made to happen. Things not just happen they are made to happen. Your wish need deliberate efforts in your part to make it happen. Obviously for your wish to come true it will require more than your efforts. But what is also obvious is that without your efforts your wishes will never come true. If you do not play your part no one – not even God your father – will be able to play your part. The reason why He created you in the first place is because he wanted you to play that part. His major contribution was to create you and deposit in you everything you need to make your wishes come to pass.

As you already know preparation takes time. If you know when you want your desire to come true you must put preparation time into account. If you are expecting a baby for example you must be aware that babies need nine months (more or less) before they can be born. You must make preparations with this truth in your mind. Too many people wait until it is too late to start making necessary preparations. Planning is a crucial component of faith.

God our father is a master of planning. He is the one who created planning. So planning is the core character of gods. He never does anything without first thinking about it and making it happen. That is why He will never do anything to you and through you without preparing you for the same. If he wants to give you something in the future He will put the desire of the same in the present.

Desire is the energy for preparation. The stronger the desire the higher the energy. Good things require intense and meticulous preparations. No wonder good things require intense desire and greater patience. You can forecast where you are going by what you are going through. I mean you can estimate the value of your future by the strength of your present desire.

KINGDOM OF GOD: REDEFINED

The core mission of Jesus was to reveal the Kingdom Of God on earth. No wonder the phrase 'kingdom of god' or 'the kingdom of heaven' anchored his conversation through out his life. Jesus has been recorded in our available biblical text mentioning this very phrase about four hundred times- many times than he mentioned any other word. He opened his public address on earth with the phrase and closed his life chapter with it. Even after his resurrection, for forty days, Jesus relentlessly continued to preach about the kingdom of God.

There is no doubt that the Kingdom of God was Jesus' life purpose. Because many people (Christians and non Christians alike) regard Jesus as their role model as well as their moral compass, the impact of His teaching is evident in our lives even to day. In my view the teaching of Jesus has had a positive impact for many –especially for people who understood it.

But many have not been able to assimilate the life changing message behind the famous phrase. As a result the teaching had had too little positive effect or had affected them in a negative way. My intention in this chapter is to explain in simple terms the message behind the Kingdom of God so that many would be able to tap into its enormous life giving potential.

Many hold a view that by the Kingdom of God (or heaven) Jesus meant the everlasting spiritual life in heaven. They believe that since Jesus' emphasis was to prepare people for the life in heaven earthly life is of less importance. For this reason many people especially those who call themselves 'Christians' pay more attention to the futuristic heavenly life and undermine the present physical bodily life.

I beg to differ. In my view this is a serious misconception of Jesus' teaching. In the following pages I will share with you the reasons why I do not believe this to be so.

To get the real picture of the Kingdom of God we will need to glean some important factual clues from the biblical texts and glue them together.

CLUE NO 1

THE KINGDOM WAS CREATED BY GOD FROM HEAVEN BUT MEANT FOR THIS WORLD

Both Jesus and John the Baptist opened their teaching by saying *repent for the Kingdom of God is near*[49].The obvious clue is that the Kingdom of God is the property of God our Father. It was designed and created by God from heaven.

The saying *the Kingdom of God is near* (or imminent) means the kingdom was coming (or had come) from another location. Jesus also dropped another hint: that the Kingdom was indeed coming from our father who lives in heaven when he taught the disciples to pray '*may your Kingdom come, may your will be done here on earth as it is in heaven'*. So we can safely say that the kingdom Jesus was referring to was made by God in heaven and was meant for this world.

CLUE NO 2

THE KINGDOM CAME WHEN JESUS STARTED TEACHING

John the Baptist started to preach by saying *repent for the Kingdom of heaven is imminently close*[50] meaning Jesus Christ, the bearer (or king) of the kingdom of heaven was indeed around the corner. John himself did not reveal the secret of the kingdom but, as the last prophet of the Old Testament, he paved the way for the arrival of the Kingdom. That is why Jesus said *since the day   John started preaching about repentance in preparation for the kingdom of God until now the kingdom of God has been advancing passionately and passionate people are taking advantage of it*[51].

But in verse 11 Jesus said *any one who is the least in the Kingdom of God is greater than John the Baptist*. By this Jesus revealed two things. First he revealed that by the time they were having this conversation the kingdom of God was already underway. Secondly Jesus pointed out that John himself – apart from preparing others for it - never experienced the Kingdom of God. As a matter of principle Jesus meant that all prophets who lived before John the Baptist did not taste the Kingdom of God.

By saying John and other prophets before him did not taste the kingdom of heaven Jesus did not imply that all of them were sinners and therefore hell bound. We know this is not true because Jesus had just said that John was the greatest of all the prophets ever lived. And we understand that many prophets who preceded John – in the likes of Moses, Abraham, Joshua and Elijah – were men of pure faith and are indeed in heaven.

Clearly then the Kingdom of God Jesus was talking about meant something different from heavenly life.

CLUE NO 3

THE KINGDOM IS EXPERIENCED IN THE MIND

After hearing Jesus talking passionately about the Kingdom of God, religious leaders wanted to know when this kingdom was expected to come and how one could recognise it. Jesus' answer to their question revealed three important facts.

 Firstly he said the Kingdom would not come by observation. Meaning it could not be seen by naked eyes. Secondly Jesus said the kingdom of God could not be physically seen at any physical geographical location. And thirdly he said the kingdom of God was already among them[52].

In all that Jesus meant to say the kingdom of God, although it was already among them and could be readily experienced, was indeed intangible. It was something that could be experienced within an individual after repentance. In other words repentance was the kingdom prerequisite. To understand the importance of this let us examine the meaning of the word repentance.

Repentance: the Kingdom Prerequisite

Adam Clarke Bible Commentary says the Greek word *metanoeite* translated as *repent* literally means *reverse of insanity (or madness).* It also means *upgrading an obsolete mindset to a sound one.*

Madness is a mental state- it is a thinking pattern that is inconsistent with a normal way of thinking. It is obsolete mental software that is incompatible with God's mental software. A religious word for madness is *sin* or *rebellion.* Paul defines sin as a thinking pattern that is inconsistent with God's way of thinking[53].

This gives us another clue that the Kingdom of God is experienced in the mind or heart. John and Jesus knew that madness and the Kingdom of God are conflicting thinking patterns that can not co-exist in one's mind. That is why before the Kingdom of God can be installed in one's mind, as Paul also indicated in the following text, madness must be uninstalled.

Do not live like other people who do not know the secret of the kingdom of God. But let God change your lifestyle by changing your thinking pattern. Only then you will be able to attest and enjoy God's perfect will for your life[54].

Repentance is a conscious wilful submission of an obsolete thinking for the purpose of being upgraded into a compatible sound thinking pattern.

CLUE NO 4

THE KINGDOM IS EXPERIENCED AFTER BELIEVING THE TEACHINGS OF JESUS

Repentance is triggered by listening and believing Jesus' principles of sound living. As we have seen in previous chapters Jesus is called the Word of God - a body of principles that forms a thinking pattern. *Accepting Jesus* means to believe the teachings (gospel) of Jesus. Accepting Jesus does not mean to become a member of a certain religion. Neither does it mean to follow or receive Jesus in the flesh. If this was the case no one could be able to do so after his death.

At one occasion Jesus referred to his flesh and blood as food for eternal life[55]. He advised who ever fancied to experience eternal life to eat his flesh and drink his blood. Understandably many, including Jesus' students, were astounded by the statement. Many more of his followers were offended to the point of deserting him altogether.

What Jesus meant to say – as he later clarified to his loyal twelve- was that his teachings about eternal sound living, if believed and acted upon, had the power to make one actually live a sound life here on earth and in eternity.

So the clue we can glean from this is that the kingdom is embedded in the teachings (words) of Jesus. It is a thinking pattern for sound living that is learnt from the teachings of Jesus.

Learning a thinking pattern is more than just listening to an eloquent religious sermon or memorising a set of complex scriptures. It is in understanding the logic- the spirit- the meaning behind the words or message that when acted upon triggers a new thinking which eventually lead to a new lifestyle. That is why Jesus said

If you continuously do what I say you will be my true disciples. And by doing so you will know the truth that will give you the freedom to enjoy sound living[56].

But to believe Jesus' word one must first believe who Jesus is. The credibility of the message is on the credibility of the messenger. It is difficult to believe the news from a distrusted source no matter how true the news might be. That is why believing in the personality of Jesus – as the son of God sent by God to teach us the principles of sound living here on earth- is a prerequisite for a sound living[57].

The Spirit is a mind installer

The *word* is a thinking pattern (or program) that needs to be installed (learnt) in one's mind. A new thinking pattern cannot be learnt without a help of a spiritual trainer – the Holy Spirit. Upon submitting our mind to him the Holly Spirit (or SNS as we discussed earlier) works with us and within us to make sure we understand and learn a new way of thinking.

The disciples of Jesus could not understand Jesus' teachings even after consistently teaching them for more than three years. That is why they needed the Spirit of Truth. As Jesus said, they needed the Spirit of Truth to coach them – elaborate and help them apply his teaching- for effective assimilation of a kingdom mentality[58].

CLUE NO 5

THE KINGDOM IS MANIFESTED IN A SOUND LIFESTYLE

Having an obsolete mind upgraded to a sound one is what Jesus termed as *to be born again*[59]. Apostle Paul calls it *'to become a new creature'.*[60] Forgiveness is a common biblical term for having a demented mind rehabilitated by learning a new Christ's thinking pattern.

In other words true repentance must lead to forgiveness. As we discussed in the earlier chapters of this book, life style is a product of a thinking pattern (or mindset). If the kingdom of God installs sound mindset then, in essence, the Kingdom leads to a sound lifestyle.

Madness leads to an evil disorganised lifestyle. People who do not live a healthy lifestyle as they should be – people like Rocham and the prodigal son – are, with all my respect, out of sanity. In other words they are ruled by the kingdom of Satan - the author of madness .That is why his kingdom is also called   the kingdom of darkness.   Jesus is the author of the Kingdom of Light. It is for this reason he cleansed (forgave) madness (sin) from people. By setting people free   from crime, poverty, sickness, and misery of all kinds, Jesus –in his own words- made the kingdom of God manifest.[61]

A sinful lifestyle (acts or behaviour) is the manifestations of sin - a sinful mindset. Most people equate pervasive behaviour such as sickness, sexual immorality and crime to sin while in effect they are the manifestations of sin. Jesus' emphasis was the principle – the thinking pattern. He knew that thoughts cause feelings and feelings leads to behaviour or lifestyle. Jesus never dealt with behaviour itself. He dealt with the root cause- the mindset. To Him behaviours such as stealing, fornication, poverty, lack of discipline and murder were just the manifestation of a sinful mentality.

Contrary to the law of Moses that demanded one must be caught in the physical act to be guilty of any sin (sexual immorality for example), Jesus said in the Kingdom of God one just need to think (hold mental images of sexual immorality) to be guilty[62]. What makes one a sinner, Jesus said is not how one acts- what or how one eats, drinks, says or wears. What makes one a sinner or otherwise is what one thinks of those actions before hand. We become sinners (insane) or righteous (wise) by the kind of thoughts we hold in our minds.[63]

Sound lifestyle in the other hand is the manifestation of a sound mind. Another word for sound living is salvation. To be saved means to experience a positive change of lifestyle through a positive change of mindset. It is a transition from a demented lifestyle into a sound lifestyle by the reason of switching from insanity to sanity. Simply put, sound living is a proof of salvation. For me it is insanity to claim that one is saved but one still manifesting an ill lifestyle. It does not make sense, for example, to say one has been saved from poverty but one still poor.

Salvation is not a heavenly phenomenon. As the bible says salvation is a hear-and-now reality. If salvation was solely meant to be an escape from a hell fire then no one could claim to be saved here on earth. We all had to wait until judgement day to find out whether we have been saved or not. Jesus with His Kingdom mission aimed at saving people. On one occasion Jesus was recorded saying that Satan's madness mission aims at stealing, killing and destroying lives. But his kingdom mission aimed at saving people- helping people switch from miserable living to living a life that is full of prosperity[64].

The Kingdom of God Is The Cause Not the Effect

As he spoke to his disciples Jesus reminded all of us that our heavenly father definitely knows we need prosperity- (plenty of nice food, houses and clothes). He made clear that it is always His ultimate pleasurable commitment to see us living in prosperity. But he went on to say that the only way to be prosperous is not by anxious toil but by understanding the secret of the Kingdom of God[65].

What this means is; the Kingdom of God itself is not prosperity but it is the cause of prosperity. Jesus meant to say that if you have the kingdom of God then you must be prosperous. This also means if you are not living in prosperity - you are constantly worried about your life and the future- you are yet to find the Kingdom of God. Just like it is impossible to have fire without heat, it is impossible to have the Kingdom of God without prosperity. Once again Jesus' emphasis is on the cause- the prosperity mentality (the Kingdom of God) and not the effects (prosperity).

The Kingdom of God is a powerful blessing that generates wealth

Moses said *God gives us the power to get wealth*[66]. Please note what he did not say. He did not say *God gives us wealth*. He meant to say

God gives us the power and it is up to us to use that power to generate wealth. Instead of giving us the wealth (the fruits) he prefers to give us the power (the seed) and teaches us how to generate wealth at will.

King Solomon also said *"the blessing of the Lord makes one rich..."*[67] David clearly differentiates between the blessing (the cause) and riches (the effect). He points out that if you have the blessing then you will inevitably end up rich. So God does not give us riches. All he does is to give us the blessing (the formula) and if we want to prosper it is our responsibility to use it to generate the product -riches.

Wisdom: The principle thing

King Solomon is arguably the   wealthiest human being ever lived. The only reason for his extraordinary achievement was wisdom -not luck or hard work. At age 17 God gave him the opportunity to ask anything (the opportunity that is given to all of us at all times). Solomon did not ask for the effects (prosperity and longevity) he went for the causes (wisdom) and he got both. No wonder he says

Joyful is the person who finds wisdom, the one who gains understanding. For wisdom is more profitable than silver, and her wages are better than gold. Wisdom is more precious than rubies; nothing you desire can compare with her. She offers you long life in her right hand, and riches and honor in her left. She will guide you down delightful paths; all her ways are satisfying. Wisdom is a tree of life to those who embrace her; happy are those who hold her tightly. By wisdom the LORD founded the earth; by understanding he created the heavens. By his knowledge the deep fountains of the earth burst forth, and the dew settles beneath the night sky[68].

Obedience: source of wisdom

According to King Solomon the source of wisdom is obedience to the divine instructions[69]. Even Jesus himself said the only way to experience the Kingdom of God is by obeying his instructions[70]. God through Isaiah the prophet said the only way to experience enjoyable prosperous life here on earth is by following divine instructions[71].

Every good thing has a way to be enjoyed. Unless one knows how to enjoy a good thing one will not be able to enjoy it. Let us say you have bought a television set for the purpose of watching your favourite programs. If you do not know how to use it you won't be able to enjoy it. Every TV from a good responsible television manufacturer comes with some instructions on how to use it. They call this the user's manual. If you ignore the user's manual for some reason there is every possibility that you won't get the pleasure out of the TV set as you should.

Life is God's product. It was meant for us His children to enjoy. The kingdom of God is the life manual. Any one who wants to enjoy life to the full can not afford to ignore it. It is on the same grounds that John the beloved student of Jesus said every one who received (believed and acted on the teaching of) Jesus became (reflected the lifestyle of the) children of God[72]. Paul also said that those who are lead by the spirit of God are the ones that experience the lifestyle that fits the child of God as He originally designed[73].

Wisdom Vs Intelligence

Wisdom is different from intelligence. Intelligence is the mental ability to understand instructions or acquire knowledge. But wisdom is the application of instruction or knowledge that solves a particular problem. When you are confronted with a difficult problem what you need is the instruction on how to solve that particular problem and apply it. Mark Murdock once said *when you ask God for a miracle he will give you an instruction.*

Those days, as we discussed earlier, God used to channel his instructions through people who had the ability to understand divine instructions. But because now every one has access to divine intelligence our Father passes information directly to our hearts. When one is confronted with any difficult situation God through SNS drops a flash of tailored instructions in a form of a creative idea that provokes a pleasant feeling.

People who achieve extraordinary results (commonly known geniuses) have developed a habit of understanding, believing and acting on divine wisdom. Geniuses are just common individuals that achieve uncommon results. They achieve uncommon results not because they follow common sense or because they have the highest IQ or because they are super humans. They achieve outstanding results because they follow the instructions from the uncommon sense.

King Solomon, it has been said, received wisdom from God and because of that he was extremely wealthy. But we have no evidence that he was given any material thing as a symbol of wisdom. What is on record however is that he always followed his heart!

Abraham blessed his son Isaac by simply making the declaration of prosperity in his life. He never gave him any inheritance in a form of material or financial wealth. But we know that Isaac was very creative and intuitive. And because of this every where he went Isaac prospered.

In his own account, Jesus did not achieve what he achieved because he was a super human. He performed miracles because he learnt the habit of following the divine instructions from His Father. And he made it clear that any one of us can do what he did (and even greater things than he did) if we can learn the secret of following our hearts[74]

Wisdom flows in the atmosphere of love

To receive wisdom the mind must be in a state of Love, relaxation, and peace .Creative ability flows best in the atmosphere of LOVE. Paul put it better when he said the Kingdom of God (wisdom) does not come (flow) by eating or drinking certain food stuff, but through the Holy Spirit that operates in the atmosphere of righteousness, peace and joy[75].

Just as fish can not live on dry land and wood can not transmit electricity, wisdom can not flow in the atmosphere of hatred, fear, worry, anxiety and confusion. Love, faith, peace and harmony are divine cables through which the Holy Spirit channels creative power.

THE KEYS OF THE KINGDOM OF GOD

And I will Give you the keys of the kingdom

Jesus Christ

A key is a symbol of authority or access. A key also stands for a secret or principle. By saying to Peter *I will give you the keys of the Kingdom of Heaven,* in a broader sense, Jesus meant to give him the secrets or principles of sound living.

Jesus used the word keys (not a key) meaning there are more than one key to the Kingdom. There are many principles that govern sound living. Sound living, like a mansion with many rooms, has a couple of aspects that each requires a different principle (wisdom) to unlock it. This includes aspects such as wellness (health and fitness), loving relationships, wealth (financial freedom), achievements, and peace of mind.

To be perfect one must be free in all these areas. A perfect person must be healthy and fit, have constant peace of mind, enjoy perfect loving relationships, attain financial freedom, and fulfil all life ambitions. In my view no human being is born perfect. We were born imperfect to be perfected. I believe the purpose of living is to learn perfection that will enable us to live a perfect life in eternity. I believe one attains perfection and is ready to pass on to eternity as soon as one fulfils a destiny. So to me life here on earth is an experimental one; it is an ongoing learning process.

Righteousness does not mean Perfection

Perfection is in successions. It is attained by learning key principles that governs each aspect of life one at a time .To be born again is a process not an event. One's mind does not get changed overnight; it takes a painstaking, time-consuming learning process. The nature and duration of the salvation process depends mainly on how severe one's mind is demented and one's co-operation with teacher Spirit.

As we have seen, to be saved one must confess and believe the personality and more importantly the teaching of Jesus on sound living. Another word for the act of confessing and believing is repentance. Repentance restores righteousness that eventually leads to salvation.

Righteousness means justification or acceptance. It also means a restoration of a relationship or communication. Demented mind disrupts communication with the Father and therefore sour the relationship. We run away from God because our minds aren't right. Not because our Father deserts us. As we have seen, God's love for us is unconditional. He loves us even when our minds aren't the best and works harder to restore our sanity.

Restoration of communication is important because teacher Spirit can not start teaching if a student is not in class or not cooperating fully. Doctor Spirit- our Father's neurosurgeon – can not start a surgical operation if the patient is not on the operating table or not co-operating fully.

Repentance is like an admission requirement. Repentance makes us the disciples (students) of The Kingdom University under professor Holy Spirit. When one repents one gets admitted into a mental rehabilitation program in the Kingdom Hospital under Dr. Holy Spirit. .That one is admitted in the rehabilitation program does not mean that one has already graduated. Just as one does not get well by being on the operating table, one does not get saved just by repenting. It takes a series of real life experiences co-ordinated by the Spirit to get our minds sorted.

One Key at a time

The keys of the kingdom are handed one at a time. I mean we do not learn all sound living principles in one go. As I said earlier perfection is a process- it happens in successions. We learn one principle at a time. As soon as we have mastered one principle we move on to learning the next one. The Spirit decides which principle one has to start with and which one should be the next. Normally he starts with one's most sensitive.

Every one of us is naturally stronger in at least one aspect of life and weaker in others. For example one might be free financially but struggle in other areas such as health or relationships. Every one of us, as the bible says, struggle with some kind of *sin that so easily trips us up*[76]. When one is free from an issue that one once struggled with (poverty for instance) it is fair to say that one is saved from poverty.

This explains why students of Jesus and other early believers struggled with character issues despite the fact that they lived with Christ in the flesh and listened to his teachings live. A chilling example is that of Judas. Despite being one of Jesus' top ministry leaders Judas struggled with financial irregularities. As a Financial Director he stole money from the Ministry Accounts and later took bribe to get his boss crucified.[77]

As a matter of fact Peter himself was still struggling with some issues at the time Jesus promised to give him the kingdom keys. For Jesus to say he will hand Peter the Kingdom Keys he signified that Peter - despite being his long time disciple -did not have the keys. And we know that Jesus did not hand in the keys to Peter until at least after his resurrection.[78] At this time Peter had a shaky faith, struggled with emotions and suffered from incredible low self esteem. No wonder soon afterwards Jesus called him Satan.[79] Just few days after his revelational confession of Jesus' divine personality Peter went on to deny Jesus three times.[80]

CLUE NO. 6

THE KINGDOM SECRET IS NOT FOR EVERY ONE

*You are permitted to understand the secret of the Kingdom of God.
But I use parables for everything I say to outsiders, so that the
Scriptures might be fulfilled: 'When they see what I do, they will learn
nothing. When they hear what I say, they will not understand.
Otherwise, they will turn to me and be forgiven.*[81]

The above text, and dozens more as we shall see, gives us another
important kingdom clue – the secret of the kingdom is exclusive to
some people. Jesus appears to suggest that God deliberately
excludes some people from understanding the secrets of the
Kingdom. Jesus under the instruction of his Father hand picked his
disciples. He chose who should follow him and turned others down
even when they offered to follow him.

For example Jesus told his twelve chosen students *"You didn't
choose me. I chose you. I appointed you to go and produce lasting
fruit..."*[82] One guy seeing Jesus picking his disciples offered to follow
him. But Jesus gave him a cold shoulder. Surprisingly, soon
afterwards Jesus found two guys who weren't particularly enthusiastic
in becoming his disciples. But Jesus actually persuaded them to join
him in preaching the kingdom of God[83]

One day Jesus told the unbelieving crowd, *"no one can come to me
unless the Father has enabled him."*[84] This clearly, as Paul also
reiterated, believing is not in the hands of a believer but in the hands
of God our Father. Paul talked extensively that understanding the
secrets of the Kingdom is a very special privilege for the few.[85] God
predetermined some people to be part of this great movement before
even they were conceived. As a matter of fact some of us were born
specifically for this purpose. For instance God told Jeremiah *"Before I
formed you in the womb I knew you, before you were born I set you
apart; I appointed you as a prophet to the nations"*[86]

The Case of Humility

Humility is in appreciating God as the source of blessings and the acceptance of the responsibility that comes with it. Humility is pure wisdom. It is understanding that sound mind and sound living is a good gift that comes from God our father. It is acknowledging the fact that who we have been, who we are and who we shall become is the manifestation of God's perfect will.

Jesus said *man shall not live by bread alone but by every word that proceeds from the mouth of God-* meaning we are alive today not because we are smart. We are living today because God planned that way.

It is always easy to brag about our achievements and blame others for their predicaments. Too often we Christians have allowed arrogance and pride to rule our hearts. As a result we tend to condemn those who are struggling with issues instead of helping them. It is difficult to love and serve people you condemn. But Paul reminds every Christian that;

> *You were dying because of your disobedience and your many sins. You used to live in sin, just like the rest of the world, obeying the devil—the commander of the powers in the unseen world. He is the spirit at work in the hearts of those who refuse to obey God. All of us used to live that way, following the passionate desires and inclinations of our sinful nature. By our very nature we were subject to God's anger, just like everyone else.*

> *But God is so rich in mercy, and he loved us so much, that even though we were dying because of our sins, he gave us life when he raised Christ from the dead. (It is only by God's grace that you have been saved!) .For he raised us from the dead along with Christ and seated us with him in the heavenly realms because we are united with Christ Jesus. So God can point to us in all future ages as examples of the incredible wealth of his grace and kindness toward us, as shown in all he has done for us who are united with Christ Jesus.*

> *God saved you by his grace when you believed. And you can't take credit for this; it is a gift from God. Salvation is not a reward for the good things we have done, so none of us can boast about it. For we are God's masterpiece. He has created us anew in Christ Jesus, so we can do the good things he planned for us long ago.*[87]

The Kingdom And The Church

Now I say to you that you are Peter (which means 'rock'), and upon this rock I will build my church, and all the powers of hell will not conquer it. And I will give you the keys of the Kingdom of Heaven. Whatever you forbid on earth will be forbidden in heaven, and whatever you permit on earth will be permitted in heaven."[88]

In my view there is a difference between the kingdom of God and the church. Jesus statement to Peter that he (Jesus) will build his church and give Peter the keys of the Kingdom suggests that the Kingdom and the church are closely related but are indeed different entities.

The church (*ekklesia* in Greek) typically means an assembly of specially chosen people. These special people are commonly known as Christians. Although a term Church is commonly used to mean a special building or group of Christians that regularly meet at a certain place its original meaning as entailed in the text is deeper than that. It appears to me that the church is a network of people who understand (or in the process of understanding) the secret of the Kingdom of God. In view of this we can say that a church is a Christian Institution whose core mission is to spread the Kingdom of God - helping people live a sound life.

The Kingdom is for Every One

The secret of the kingdom is for a chosen few but the kingdom of God it self is for every one. I mean God want every human being to live a sound life but not every one will know the dynamics of sound living. We do not need to be electronic engineers to enjoy electronic equipments. I mean one does not need to know how the television is made before enjoying watching favourite Tv programs. Likewise people do not need to be Christians to enjoy sound living.

Christians are Jesus' staff recruited in his ministry (the church) for the purpose of dispensing sound living in the world. They are part of a medical team working in the Kingdom Hospital. The Kingdom Hospital (the church) is for any one who needs health (the kingdom /sound living). But one does not need to be part of a Kingdom Hospital staff to get health.

Like any Institution, the Kingdom of God has many different branches, departments, and wings. Paul says although all Christians are members of the Church they hold different responsibilities. The Holy Spirit is the Kingdom Chief Executive. His job is to represent, direct and execute Jesus' interests on earth. This includes, of course recruiting and managing kingdom staff. The Holy Spirit recruits some of us as doctors, accountants, artists, lawyers, preachers, and thinking teachers to mention but a few.[89]

Locking and Unlocking

By saying "...*whatever you forbid (lock) on earth will be forbidden (locked) in heaven, and whatever you permit (unlock) on earth will be permitted (unlocked) in heaven.*" Jesus meant to give Peter, as the first Leader of the Church, the authority to make decisions that would affect the every day running of a church.

Leaders and staff need training before they can be trusted with any authority to make decisions in the organisation. That is why Peter and other eleven disciples had to undergo a three-and-a-half year training program before they could be trusted to dispense the principles of sound living. Peter's leadership training was even more intense because he was being prepared to be the top leader.

This, of course, does not mean that the church has the authority to admit or exclude people from going to heaven. Yes they might make decisions that might affect other people's lives here on earth. Each individual church wing or department have the right to form tailored regulations to suit their mission here on earth. But neither the church nor her leaders have a say on who should make heaven and who should go to hell.

In fact even Jesus himself had no authority over the selection of his own disciples. He did not just go around and randomly hand pick any one he liked. But, he says, every disciple was brought to him by His father[90]. This is because, in his own words, the Kingdom is his Father's business[91]. So he chose every disciple under the direction of his Father. That is why he couldn't even guarantee who would join him at the high table at the Kingdom banquet[92].

It makes a perfect sense there fore to say that John the Baptist and all other prophets before him –including Abraham, Isaac, Jacob, Moses, Joshua and Elijah- were non Christians. They were not part of the church of Jesus Christ because the church started after many of them had long died. Although they believed in the coming messiah they did not live long enough to see him and be part of his ministry. And as said earlier John was not part of the kingdom because he had his own separate ministry and had his own staff (disciples). This also means that there are a lot of people who are serving God in many different capacities who are not (and will never be) Christians!

Salvation and Christianity

To be saved is different from being a Christian. As discussed, salvation is deliverance from a life predicament. That one is saved does not necessarily mean that one is a Christian. A good example is that of a man I have nick named the Legion Man.[93] Having a legion of madness demons casted out of his mind the Legion Man offered to follow Jesus and become one of his disciples. But Jesus reclined his offer and asked him to go home instead.

That one has been delivered from a certain problem does not mean that one has an obligation to become a Church member. Yes Jesus used deliverance as a way of recruiting his staff and he still does. But not every disciple was recruited after being delivered. In other words one can be saved without becoming a Christian. And one can become a Christian without being saved. But one can not remain a Christian without being saved in some degree at some point.

Jesus saved people from their predicaments because he wanted them to be free- not because he wanted them to be Christians. He saves people because he is a saviour. As a saviour his main job is to save full stop! Many times we pastors want to use helping people as Church membership recruitment tool. We assume that people must become members of our congregation because they have been delivered through our ministry. As a junior pastor I used to be very frustrated to minister to people and those same people snub my church. It was even more frustrating when the people I have spent my valuable resources in helping recover fail to even appreciate my service. Thank God I later came to understand that I was the Kingdom employee. My job was to serve people and my pay was to come from my employer- Jesus Christ.

Church Responsibility

Responsibility is response to ability. Every privilege comes with responsibility. The main purpose of a church is to dispense the Kingdom of God -sound living principles. Our responsibility as Christians is to help people live a sound life not to recruit church members. Jesus commanded His disciples to go and dispense life to all creatures every where. He meant to take care of all people regardless of their religious, sexual or social economic background.

We are saved to save others. The very reason we have been strengthened is to strengthen the weak. Jesus told Simon Peter
"Simon, Simon, Satan has asked to sift you as wheat. But I have prayed for you, Simon, that your faith may not fail. And when you have turned back, strengthen your brothers."[94]

Another word for 'god' is *leader* or *provider*. So Christians have been entrusted with an exclusive access to extra abundance because God expect them to take care of those who cannot take care of themselves. This includes children and people with severe special needs. Speaking to the leaders, God said; *...I say you are gods. I chose you to be leaders and commissioned you to take charge of my people in my behalf .Your responsibility was to care for the weak and the destitute; defend the rights of the poor ; stand up for the powerless, and prosecute all those who exploit them. But it seems you have lost the vision of your core mission. It is clear to me that you have lost the sense of purpose. Because of this your world is crushing around you and you are heading for a shameful destruction...95*

LOVE: THE KINGDOM MASTER KEY

Three things will last forever—faith, hope, and love—and the greatest of these is love

---

1 Corinthians 13:13

So far we have discussed that *Kingdom keys* stand for the principles of sound living. They are called keys because they are many. As a matter of fact these keys are not new. They have been around since the world begun. Over the years different peoples and cultures have managed to get a glimpse of each principle.

The nation of Israel was the first nation on earth to have them in one bunch; in a more tailored, compact and systematic way. These principles were given to the people by God through their leader Moses. This set of principles (or law) was called the Law of Moses or Torah. The Law of Moses comprised hundreds of laws. The Jewish people were obliged to live by all these laws. The quality of a Jewish life was determined by how one obeyed the Law of Moses.

What make the principles of the Kingdom of God as taught by Jesus more effective is their simplicity and practicability.

By simplicity I mean Jesus summarised the laws of sound living into just one main law divided into two or three sub laws. Not only that Jesus summarise the law but he also brought the dimension of the Holy Spirit to install the laws directly into people's minds for easy implementation. Now the question is this; what is that one fundamental key?

Asked by one of the doctors of the Law of Moses as to which Law is superior in the Law of Moses Jesus said;

'You must love the LORD your God with all your heart, all your soul, and all your mind.' This is the first and greatest commandment. A

second is equally important: 'Love your neighbor as yourself.' The entire law and all the demands of the prophets are based on these two commandments.[96]

Loving God does not mean to follow a set of rules or join a religion. Obeying God simply means obeying His instructions as dispensed by the spirit. In a practical sense Loving God means fulfilling God's purpose for your life. Loving other people as yourself means using your endowed resources to help others (especially people in severe needs) live a life you would like to live yourself.

Generally speaking Love is the Kingdom master key. Jesus calls it *the royal law* and James calls it *the law of freedom* or simply *the golden law.* Jesus made it clear that all what the Law of Moses and the prophets taught could be summed up in one word - Love. This is because God is love and every one who has the spirit (nature) of God must be in love. Meaning any one who claims to have known God must love himself and other people especially those who are in need[97]. James the blood brother of Jesus even concluded that the only religion that is true, pure and acceptable to God is to live according to the golden law of loving others as oneself[98].

Paul puts it best by plainly and strongly stating that Love is the master key to the Kingdom of God[99]. He said nothing holds true everlasting spiritual, psychological and material value as love.

In summary the golden rule demands that we use our God given resources in fulfilling our life purpose of improving our own life and the life of others in our community.

Eternal Life

I believe the phrase 'eternal life' has a deeper meaning than just being eternally alive. We know that every human soul will live for ever. But there will be two kinds of lifestyles in eternity. One is that filled with pain, anguish and misery in a place popularly referred to as hell and the other is that which is littered with love, joy and prosperity in a place popularly referred to as paradise. This latter kind of life is what people in the bible days referred to as 'eternal life'.

Eternal life means a never ending enjoyable life   made in heaven but meant for and starts here on earth and spills over into eternity. By enjoyable life I mean the life that is satisfied with spiritual and bodily needs; needs such as wellness, love, material wealth, achievements and inner peace.

As we have seen sacred texts tell us that God's plan was and still is to make human beings rule THE WORLD not heaven. Heaven is God's throne, but the world is OUR throne. King David said[100] *Heaven belongs to God our Father but He has given the earth to us (His children) to take full control of it.*

IN CONCLUSION

In the light of what we have seen, The Kingdom of God stands for *The Principles of Eternal Sound Living*. The Church is the ministry of Jesus Christ with a sole purpose of programming peoples' minds for a sound living that starts here on earth and rolls over into eternity. [101] The kingdom of God is a doctrine that installs a thinking pattern that empowers us to live a prosperous living here on earth.[102]

Jesus' mission was to spread the kingdom of God here on earth- not to take people to heaven. His main message was a sound living here on earth and beyond. No wonder He taught His disciples to keep on praying for God's Kingdom to come here on earth and that His will of a prosperous living be fulfilled HERE ON EARTH as it is in heaven[103].

Heaven is God's palace. Just as a palace is the king's (or queen's) residence and office, heaven is God's residence and office. Because his family was expanding He created this world to be a new home (or palace) for His children. A home that will give his children the freedom to live a life of their liking as it is in their father's heaven. Jesus came to teach people how to enjoy their lives here on earth to the full as they prepare to continue to do so in to eternity!

For those of us who were created and called to carry on the mission of Jesus Christ let us remember that our mission is to teach and inspire people to enjoy their living on earth. We must not forget that the golden rule for enjoyable living is Love- the love of God, the love of self and the love of others.

'GOD' IS YOUR FAMILY NAME

For I have come to seek and save the lost; I came so that all people may have life full of abundant prosperity

---

Jesus Christ

Charles Clements was the 5th and last Earl of Leitrim Ireland. Since he had no child he chose his brother Hon. Francis Patrick Clements to be his heir presumptive. But in 1907 Francis Clements mysteriously disappeared.

According to New York Times of March 8 1908 Clements moved to New York where he worked as a stoker. Due to deteriorating health caused by hardships in the city he later moved to Kansas City where he hired a room in one of the city lodgings. "During his stay at the lodging house", the paper reports, "Francis pawned nearly all of his personal effects. He was taken ill of pneumonia and moved to a General Hospital where he died without telling anything further of himself. He went under the name of Herbert Domican"

Charles Clements spent thousands of dollars trying to establish his brother's whereabouts. After a meticulous search, Herbert's picture was luckily recognized by one of the maids at the lodging he last hired a room. When the body of Herbert Domican was exhumed it was correctly identified to be that of Francis Patrick Clements. With no heir, the Earldom of Leitrim became extinct upon the Earl's death in 1952.

You are heir of your father's mega wealth. But you, like Francis Patrick Clements, might be unaware of who you really are. Instead you have allowed your unfortunate circumstances to define who you are. Circumstances like poverty, sickness, divorce, criminality, and failure have become your family name. May be your names have been replaced by a prison number. You are no longer treated like a proper dignified human being. Please allow me to remind you that your name is not that which you have been wrongly given by men. You are a precious lovely child of our father God. And if your God is your real father you belong to a Godly family. I mean your real family name is GOD.

Too often we get lost in our ignorance, insecurities, guilt and fear. We beat ourselves in agony and frustration thinking that we do not deserve anything good from God. Many times we estimate our worth by the way other people treat us. But the truth is that our worth is in God who created us.

Few days ago I was listening to one of my favorite preachers -Pastor Joel Osteen. In the course of his sermon he brought up a telling story that immensely boosted my self esteem. As he was visiting his friend's house Pastor Osteen saw a picture hanged on the wall. In his judgment, the picture was less impressive and didn't deserve to be on any of the walls of such a magnificent house.

To his amazement he later learnt that the picture was an original work of a famous artist Pablo Picasso and his friends had paid one million (US) dollars for it. What made the picture so valuable was not necessarily the work itself but the value of the painter. The portrait carried the authentic personal Picasso signature.

What makes you so valuable is not necessarily the way you look but the value and purpose of your creator. People may have their own opinion about you but the fact is you are the work of God the almighty. He created you the way He wanted you to be and put His own signature in you- HIS LIFE. Your spirit is God's seal of ownership. Your unique DNA label is a proof that you were exclusively made in heaven for a unique purpose. As long as you are still alive you still have a purpose on earth.

To the world you might be one person but to God you mean the world. He can't afford to lose you that's why He sent our brother Jesus Christ to seek and save us. Understanding your value, Jesus laid down his life for you. He lived and died to remind you that we are still the sons of God. His sole purpose of enduring the cross was to bring us back to the awareness of who we really are and enjoy our deserved life on earth.

I repeat, Jesus was not a religious man. He never came to start a religion or make people religious. Jesus did not come to take people to heaven. He came to help people live a better life here on earth. He came for ordinary people who have lost the sense of identity and purpose. And so is this book. I have written this book not for the purpose of trying to persuade you to join a Christian religion or indeed any other religion. I want you to know that you, the way you are- nothing more nothing less- are the child of the most high God. If you are not happy with your life the way it is be assured that you deserve better.

Many people believe God can take them to a luxurious eternal life in heaven but do not believe the same God can give them a better life here on earth. In my judgment a good eternal life is more expensive than the life here. Before we can believe Him for a heavenly life, God challenged us to try Him for a better life here and now.

No matter how bad your current situation might be you can still live the life you have always desired. All you need to do is to believe. Believe that you deserve that life and exercise your faith as you have learnt in this book. No mistake of the past can cancel your inheritance. Your inheritance is still waiting for you to come back into your senses and claim it. If you won't claim it no one else will.

I was reading a book recently and stumbled on something like this *"This world is full of good things and some of them have your name on it. All you need to do is to locate them and order them"*. I had long desired a black automatic ML version of a Mercedes Benz but thought it was well too expensive and too good for me. Having read this my desire for ML was rekindled and I started to exercise my faith immediately. Within three weeks I was a proud owner of my dream car. Amazingly enough, when my wife was reading the car registration documents she noticed that the car was actually registered here in England on my birthday!

I believe you are one of the people destined for greatness. Many people, according to the statistics, never read pass the first page of any book. For you to be still reading this last paragraph shows that you are heading for a spectacular life. I mean you have heard your destiny calling your real name and responded. Only you can testify how many hardships you have endured to be where you are. It is for this reason I confidently say that you have a great future ahead of you. Your life still has a greater meaning than anyone can imagine.

Thank you very much for taking time to read this book. I hope you have been inspired enough to start enjoying the rest of your living here on earth because you are well worth it!

We are gods

ABOUT THE AUTHOR

Rev. Noel Maturlu who lives in England is a founder and Executive Director of Dream Life Mission. He is lucky to be married to a beautiful wife Sheyla and together they have been blessed with two lovely daughters (Klerios and Charity) and a wonderful son- Adili.

If you have comments or questions please feel free to contact Rev. Noel through this email address: noel@dreamlifemission.com

We are gods

REFERENCES

[1] *Western Christian biblical references Psalm 93:1, Psalm 96:10, and 1 Chronicles 16:30 include (depending on translation) text stating that "the world is firmly established, it cannot be moved." In the same tradition, Psalm 104:5 says, "the LORD set the earth on its foundations; it can never be moved." Further, Ecclesiastes 1:5 states that "And the sun rises and sets and returns to its place" (From http://en.wikipedia.org/wiki/Galileo_Galilei) .*

2 Psalms 82:1-6

3 Genesis 1:26-28

4 Psalms 8:4-8

5 Genesis 2:7

6 Genesis 1:26-28

7 Galatians 4:1- 7

8 Luke 15:11-32

9 Hebrews 5:8

10 Romans 8:38-39

11 Genesis 47-50

12 Nu 13:33

13 1John 5:8

14 Acts 2

15 Joel 2:28

16 Hebrews 8:10-11

17 John 4:21-24

18 Titus 2:11-12

19 Phil 2:13

20 Jeremiah 29:11

---

21 Psalms 37:4

22 James 1:17

23 Allan Cohen, Relax into wealth

24 Acts 20:32-35

25 Genesis 1:3

[26] *John 1:1-4, 10, 14*
27 Eph. 3:20

28 John 16:24

29 Matt 7:7-8

30 Matt 6:8

31 Matt 8:5-13

32 Mark 5:9-13

33 Job 1:9; 2:4-6

34 Luke 22:31

35 Numbers 21:1-9

36 Proverbs 16:1

37 Habakkuk 2:2

38 Exodus 31:18; 32:16

39 Numbers 13: 17-20

40 Joshua 1:3- 4

41 Genesis 30:37-39

42 1Tim 4:8

43 Philippians 3:7-8

44 1Sam 17:25-30

45 Judges 14-15

46 Heb. 11:6

47 Mathew 19:27-29

48 Hebrews 12:1-2

---

49 Matt.3:2; 4:17; Mark 1:15

50 Matt. 3:1-3

51 Matt. 11:12

52 Luke 17:20-21

53 Romans 14:23

54 Romans 12:2

55 John 6:51-68

56 John 8:32-33

57 Romans 10:9-10

58 John 16:7-15

59 John 3:3

60 2Co 5:17

61 Matt 12:28

62 Mt 5:27-28

63 Matt 15:10-20

64 John 10:10

65 Luke 12:22-32

66 Deuteronomy 8:18

67 Proverbs 10:22

68 Proverbs 3:13-20

69 Proverbs 1:7

70 Math 7:21

71 Isaiah 1:19

72 John 1:12

73 Romans 8:14

74 John 14:10-12; Heb. 5:8-9

75 Romans 14:17

---

76 Heb. 12:1

77 John 12:6

78 John 21:15-19

79 Lu 4:8

80 Matthew 26:31-75

81 Mark 4:11-12

82 John 15:16

83 Luke 9:57-62

84 John 6:44,65

85 Romans chapter 9

86 Jeremiah 1:5

87 Ephesians 2:1-10

88 Matthew 16:18-19

89 Romans 12:3-13; 1Corithians 12:1-31

90 John 6:44, 65; 17:6-10

91 Lu 2:49

92 Matt. 20:20-23

93 Mark 5:19

94 Luke 22:31-32

95 Psalms 82:1-8

96 Matthew 22:37-40

97 1John 2:1-11

98 James 1:17

99 1Corithians 13

100 Psalms 115:16

101 Luke 4: 18-19 and John 10:10

102 Titus 2:11-12

We are gods

---

103 Matt. 6:10